PLAYING IN THE BAND

An Oral and Visual Portrait of the

GRATEFUL DEAD

PLAYING IN THE BAND

by David Gans and Peter Simon

Foreword by Phil Lesh

HERBIE GREENE

St. Martin's Griffin
New York

For C.J.P.

—D.G.

For Ronni

—P.S.

PLAYING IN THE BAND: AN ORAL AND VISUAL PORTRAIT OF THE GRATEFUL DEAD. Text copyright © 1985, 1996 by David Gans. New photographs and compilation of pre-existing photographs copyright © 1985 by Peter Simon. All rights reserved. Printed in the United States of America. No part of this book may be used or reproduced in any manner whatsoever without written permission except in the case of brief quotations embodied in critical articles or reviews. For information, address St. Martin's Press, 175 Fifth Avenue, New York, N.Y. 10010.

Produced by March Tenth, Inc.

Design by Chic Ago

Composition by Folio Graphics Co. Inc.

Library of Congress Cataloging-in-Publication Data

Gans, David.
    Playing in the band : an oral and visual portrait of the Grateful Dead / by David Gans and Peter Simon.
        p.   cm.
    Reprint. Originally published: New York : St. Martin's Press, 1985.
        ISBN 0-312-14391-5
        1. Grateful Dead (Musical Group)   2. Rock musicians—Biography.
    I. Simon, Peter.
    ML421.G72G3   1996
    782.42166'092'2—dc20
    [B]   96-13307
                                               CIP
                                                MN

First published in Great Britain by the Penguin Group

First St. Martin's Griffin Edition: July 1996

10 9 8 7 6 5 4 3 2 1

Contents

FOREWORD

In our so-called global village, where even the devil is only famous for fifteen minutes, it may no longer be possible for the *solitary* artist to make an impact on his world unaided. But who's to say a spaceship isn't high art? How about a gothic cathedral, or an artificial heart or an eighty-foot racing schooner or an NFL pass play? Or even playing in the band?

When the Grateful Dead is *happening,* it happens to everyone in attendance, band and audience. So in a sense, we're *all* playing in the band.

I see it as a metaphor for humanity: Didn't Ben Franklin say something about hanging together or hanging separately?

Grateful Dead is more than music, but it has always been *fundamentally* music. *Playing in the Band* is a report on this ongoing experiment in collective creativity.

—Phil Lesh
San Rafael, California
January 1985

PREFACE

Playing in the Band is not intended as a history of the Grateful Dead, as a social phenomenon nor as a musical endeavor. To my mind, the most fascinating—and most often overlooked—aspect of the Dead phenomenon is the sophisticated and unique musical language that has evolved among these players in their two decades together. The Dead sprang from the "Summer of Love," but they are not a "sixties band" preserving the music of a bygone era. They are a progressive ensemble whose ambitious, eclectic, and anarchic method was *established* in the sixties but whose sound is always being updated, not in response to contemporary styles but to the ever-changing relationships between these six very different people.

The "dialogue" in this book is for the most part assembled from separate interviews, although some passages actually did come from conversations with more than one subject. My purpose in presenting the Grateful Dead this way is not to create the illusion of six musicians sitting in a room together, but to show the similarities and differences among the band members and allow each to contribute to the whole in his own voice—as it is in the music of the Dead—rather than impose a single narrative voice over theirs.

The lyrics quoted herein are all from Grateful Dead songs, and their sources are deliberately unidentified. Seeing these words outside their usual contexts, the reader may find new angles from which to engage the ideas and images.

—D.G.

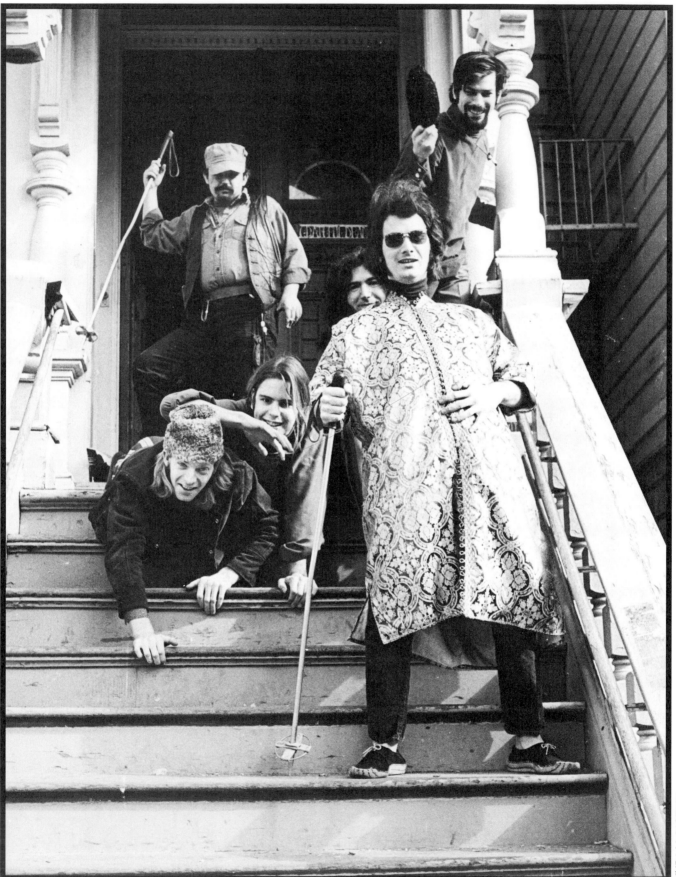

ACKNOWLEDGMENTS

Much of my understanding of the musical workings of the Grateful Dead is based on what I've learned from playing Dead-inspired music, most of it with the same group of players for more than a decade of breakups and breakthroughs, volume wars and high times. To fellow players in the band past and present—Steve Horowitz, Bob Nakamine, Alan Feldstein, Tom Yacoe, Jerry Horn, Michael Shaw, and Ernie Yoshioka—my love and gratitude for all the truth and fun we've shared. The one immutable truth, the *only* rule that has refused to bend, is that the best way to ensure a magical session is to leave the tape recorders at home.

People have been taking tape recorders to Dead shows since the band started, and the well-annotated tape collections of "aural historians" Lou Tambakos and Bob Menke were indispensable reference sources in the preparation of this book. Both of these men gave generously of their time, tapes, and notes; when I needed to know when a certain song made its first appearance, or how often Pigpen played "Katie Mae," for example, Lou and/or Bob came through with the information and—more often than not—the tape to prove it. I am also grateful to Michael Dolgushkin, who compiled a comprehensive book of Dead gigs and song lists.

Invaluable assistance was also provided by historian Dennis McNally, who graciously made available a few well-chosen items from his research for a history of the Dead; Blair Jackson and Regan McMahon, who aided the cause as friends, Deadheads, and fellow journalists; Paul Grushkin, editor of *The Official Book of the Dead Heads* and general manager of the Bay Area Music Archive, who shared his photo connections; Eileen Law of the Grateful Dead office, my first friend in the organization and a steady source of encouragement and guidance.

We are thankful to all the photographers, but most especially to Mary Ann Mayer, Herbie Greene, John Werner, and Andy Leonard for making their entire collections available to our rapacious eyeballs. Assistance in acquiring photographs was also provided by Eric Colby, Tita Bailey, Brian Connor, Jerilyn Brandelius, Sharon Dumont, Dave Zimmer, Ron Delany, Amy Bursten, and Richard Russo.

◆   ◆   ◆

ON THE STEPS OF 710 ASHBURY STREET, SAN FRANCISCO, CIRCA 1967. PIGPEN IS AT UPPER LEFT. *FROM LOWER LEFT:* PHIL LESH, BOB WEIR, JERRY GARCIA, BILL KREUTZMANN, MICKEY HART.

Acknowledgments

Original, unpublished interview material was provided by Rip Rense, Jon Sievert, Vic Garbarini, Peter Simon, Miles Hurwitz, Blair Jackson, Mary Eisenhart, and Wendy Goldstein and Linda Ellerbee of NBC News. Spectacular caches of clippings came from Zohn Artman, Ren Grevatt, and Robert McNamara. Very special assistance in getting this project off the ground came from Julie Milburn, Alan Trist, Rock Scully, and Ben Fong-Torres.

Mary Eisenhart contributed endless hours of typing, reading, philosophizing, and encouragement out of the kindness of her heart and her love for the subject matter. Susan Dobra also logged a healthy share of typewriter time and gave much literary assistance.

Grateful Dead staff and crew members John Cutler, Harry Popick, Dan Healy, Steve Parish, Eileen Law, Ram Rod, Robbie Taylor, and Bear sat still for interviews; Kidd Candelario, Joe Thomas, Paul Roehlk, Billy Bullshit, Willy Legate, Brian Williams, and Howard Danchik, Don Pearson, and Bernie Granat tolerated my presence underfoot at shows and at the studio.

Danny Rifkin and Sue Stephens of the Dead organization assisted in their special ways, as did staff members Janet Soto, Maruska Greene, Sue Gottlieb, Mary Jo Meinolf, Bonnie Parker, and Steve Marcus, a friend since our BASS days.

John Barlow offered invaluable guidance in dealing with this occasionally frustrating crowd. His perspective helped me organize and interpret my observations, and his friendship gave me confidence. Thanks also to Jill Johnson for moral support and great good humor.

Material and/or spiritual support was given by Lorraine Acuña, Wendy Brooks, Lee Edmond, Steve Gayle, Valerie Gilbert, Mick Jones, Kevin Laffey, Dick Latvala, Barbara Lewit, Pat Mathews, John and Helen Meyer, Hale Milgrim, Jan Olsen, Karen Parisi, Hillel Resner, Sandy Rosen, Goldie Rush, David Russell, Lori Schifrin, Larry Stein, Steven Walstead, and Barbara Whitestone.

Bill Graham and his company—especially Bob Barsotti, Sherry Wasserman, Colleen Kennedy, and Jan Simmons—have been instrumental in some of the highest times I (and thousands of other Deadheads, and rock fans in general) have ever had. Thank you for all the years of safe and comfortable shows as well as for your specific help with this book.

G. Brown, fellow journalist and AMC-head, helped me out in ways he'll never know.

David McGee, managing editor of *Record,* not only taught me a great deal about my craft but also waited patiently for me to come back to work. So did my employers at *Mix,* David Schwartz and Penny Jacob. My friends and colleagues there let me know I still belonged, and they tolerated my repeated failure to return the typewriter on time.

Thanks to our editor, Bob Miller, for his patience in seeing this project through many delays and upheavals. Chance (and Barry Fey) put us together in Jamaica, and Bob's confidence and generosity took it from there. Thanks also to Marta Miller for her grace and understanding.

Sandra Choron, agent and producer, has been a patient teacher, deliverer of well-timed kicks in the ass, and a good friend through my first book experience. If I'm very lucky, I'll never have to find out how other agents operate. Thanks for the referral, Mr. Marsh.

It was Stephen Donnelly who dragged me kicking and screaming to my first Grateful Dead show, on March 5, 1972, and thereby changed my life for good and for keeps. Thanks, S.J.

And Carolyn Jones Paolino, my best friend in life, strongest supporter, and most valued critic—I love you best of all.

—D.G.

Introduction
MORE THAN HUMAN

"Verbal communication is open to interpretation, just like the songs are. I've prefaced interviews in the past by saying that I can't do anything but lie. All talk is lying, and I'm lying now. And that's true, too. Go hear me play. That's me—that's what I have to say. That's the form my thoughts have taken." —JERRY GARCIA

"Once in a while you can get
       shown the light
In the strangest of places
If you look at it right"

GARCIA: You have to get past the idea that music has to be any *one* thing. To be alive in America is to hear all kinds of music constantly. Radio, records, churches, cats on the street— everywhere music, man. And with records, the whole history of music is open to anyone who wants to hear it.

Maybe Chuck Berry was the first rock musician because he was one of the first blues cats to listen to records, so he wasn't locked into the blues idiom. Nobody has to fool around with musty old scores, weird notation, and scholarship bullshit. You can just go into a record store and pick a century, pick a country, pick *anything* and dig it, make it a part of you, add it to the stuff you carry around, and see that it's all music.

"The shape it takes
Could be yours to choose"

GARCIA: Coming to see the Grateful Dead is like getting a kit from Radio Shack—

WEIR: Yeah. The audience gets to help put it together.

GARCIA: And it might not work.

HART: Each night we have to find out for ourselves what the Grateful Dead is.

GARCIA: You can't really refer to previous gigs. It's almost like starting over again every night.

We start with things that make basic musical sense and . . . kind of go through our own personal musical evolution *as we recall it that night.*

"See here how everything
Lead up to this day"

GARCIA: What we've been going after all along is still working for us. . . . It has to do with the idea that you can go out and truly try to invent music and get somewhere special every time you play. And it happens.

The standard show-biz formula that says you have to repeat your most successful gesture seems to eat up performers very fast. Musicians buy that and they burn out, lose interest in music—and it's understandable. It's very hard to play exactly the same thing night after night without getting terribly bored.

"Feel your way, like the day before"

GARCIA: We have an audience that doesn't insist that we play our hits or anything like that. They come for the unique experience of the music that happens *that* time. This has been very liberating to us as musicians, because it's let it continue to be interesting.

KREUTZMANN [1966]: We just play what we want to play, what we personally like. There's five different musicians and five different tastes. We try to encompass each taste as best we can. They blend pretty well.

HART: You bring the best parts of yourself to it and you see how it goes with everybody else. You have to compromise, surrender—give yourself up to it. It's more than you—it's a collective entity, something we all have made. When it works right it can be special. When it's not right, when there's a conflict of ideas, it won't be as easy to listen to. But it is *life,* man. Nobody is "on" every day, but we're always up there trying.

Do you pattern your music at all according to what you think the audience wants to hear?

GARCIA: Never. It has to come from us.

WEIR: We leave things awfully loose. A lot of people just naturally don't like things that loose—in life, art, music. God knows they're entitled to their tastes, as we're entitled to ours.

MYDLAND: When I first joined [in 1979], I learned the songs by listening to the albums. When I started playing them live, they said, "Well, it doesn't go like that anymore. . . ." So I wound up learning the songs twice.

14

AN OUTDOOR GIG WITH THE "WALL OF SOUND" PA, 1974

BOB MARKS

Any other band I've been in has rehearsed over and over, grinding it into the ground. I'm glad we don't, but we could use a *little* more rehearsal. . . . I don't think we've ever run through a song more than four or five times before playing it.

Do you get told what to do very much?

MYDLAND: No. And I'm starting to get used to it.

WEIR: We may not be the most professional outfit on the face of the planet, but once things get rolling, there is *something* that happens.

LESH: Sometimes it sputters and won't start, but when it pays off——

GARCIA: It comes up triple bars. All the golden yummies.

LESH: For a short time.

GARCIA: For *seconds* on end!

◆　◆　◆

When the Grateful Dead played a series of concerts at Berkeley's Greek Theatre the weekend before the opening of the Democratic National Convention in July of 1984, news people drifted over from San Francisco to pick up a bit of local color. Most of the television reports on the Dead began with a brief shot of the stage and/or a closeup of Jerry Garcia playing his guitar, then turning to the audience, zeroing in on the tie-dyed clothing and unkempt hair, Volkswagen vagabonds and backpacking hitchhikers, hypnotic drug fumes and blissful smiles. Fifteen years after Woodstock, the news people said, a Grateful Dead concert is the last bastion of hippiedom.

The name Grateful Dead is used to conjure up images of a lifestyle that's as passé as the word *lifestyle* itself. The American media treat the Dead as though they were some kind of "Haightland" traveling theme park, re-creating the "groovy vibes" of the Summer of Love at fifteen bucks a pop.

As widespread as the Grateful Dead's reputation is, very little is known about the band's music in mainstream America because their music is hardly ever played on the radio. The rock press rarely covers the Dead, and pop critics assigned to their concerts almost always find it easier to report on the Grateful Dead *phenome-*non—that colorful, anachronistic throng dancing strangely to the strains of this sound so devoid of gesture, backbeat, and flash.

Most reviews deal only with the reflection of the Dead's music in its audience when they deal with the music at all, because it's damned hard music to get a handle on. In *The New Rolling Stone Record Guide*, critic Dave Marsh called the Grateful Dead "nostalgia mongers" and likened them to the Beach Boys in "offering facile reminiscence to an audience with no memory of its own."

"I have always been amazed that more people don't take advantage of this very inexpensive medicine."
—BILL GRAHAM

The Beach Boys had years and years of success as a recording act before they lost the songwriting and producing services of their insane visionary, Brian Wilson. It wasn't until they tired of failing with new records that they relegated themselves to repeating their most successful music again and again.

15

". . . I'M STARTING TO GET USED TO IT."

DAVID GANS

MARY ANN MAYER

THE BAND'S FIRST GOLD RECORD, FOR THE LIVE LP *GRATEFUL DEAD*, AWARDED IN 1972

16

The Grateful Dead *can't* cash in on their glory days, because they never had any—at least in the commercial sense. Their records rarely come within shouting distance of the Top 10, but since 1967 they have released eighteen albums totaling twenty-five discs, more then twenty-five solo albums and spinoff projects, plus compilations, LPs of early concert recordings, video projects, and a concert movie.

They became popular in the days of "underground" music, and they have remained essentially an "underground" sensation for twenty years. *Twenty years* of earning their living on the road because their records rarely do better than break even but their concerts are a hot ticket wherever they go; of giving a small but quite ample segment of the populace what it wants by playing what they want the only way they know how. I tell you, there is something more to the Grateful Dead "phenomenon" than the "lifestyle" baggage they drag through their existence.

That something is music. Many Deadheads are less concerned with music than with the ambiance and sense of community they find at Dead concerts, and doubtless a sizeable number of fans are unconcerned with the subtleties and sophistication of the sound. But music, not lifestyle, is central to the Grateful Dead; if playing in the band didn't continue to challenge and reward them, these people wouldn't have kept at it for so long.

"What we are is artists trying to survive in that half-world of entertainment which is more conscious of its entertainment self than it is of its artist self," says Jerry Garcia, the band's lead guitarist and reluctant guru to the Deadheads.

"We're overnight failures who have stuck with it," adds Bob Weir, who has been playing guitar together with Garcia since he was seventeen years old. "We're the exception to just about every rule in the entertainment business."

The Dead are the only band left in America

PETER SIMON

beyond the menu of romance, lust, salesmanship, and self-congratulation available at most rock concerts.

And more important, there are long passages in each concert during which they aren't playing any song at all. This is "the part that's *really* the show," according to Garcia, when the musicians go exploring together and invent new things by abandoning formal structures and searching for new ways to "make one instrument out of many," as Weir puts it.

The Dead play their sets almost entirely without narration or cheerleading. The most you'll get between songs is usually a cryptic remark that is probably the punch line to some backstage joke—and which, if repeated, soon becomes the audience's joke as well.

The music is very much a function of the players' temperaments. It's fun to listen to them converse instrumentally—to argue, persuade, suggest, chide, needle, and affirm. Personalities have *everything* to do with it: You can discern each player's mood from the notes he plays and how he responds to the others—or you think you can, and that works just as well.

that's still playing improvisational music on any meaningful scale. "It's an inescapable part of what we do," Garcia pointed out in a 1981 interview. "It isn't exactly in the forefront of what's going on in music, because all the pop trends have been for songs—catchy shit."

The Dead are not now nor have they ever been a rock and roll band in the entertainment industry sense; they avoid most of the show-biz routines that characterize big-time rock today. Rather than rehearse *a* show and play it more or less identically throughout a tour, the Dead draw on an active repertoire of nearly a hundred titles and vary the content and contour from show to show.

"We don't make up our sets beforehand," said Garcia in 1966, and it's still the case. "We'd rather work off the tops of our heads than off a piece of paper." The sequence of songs in each Dead set describes a progression of emotional tones conveying a complex set of feelings ranging

"Our first responsibility is to amuse ourselves. If we can't do that, then we can't entertain anyone." —BOB WEIR

"People come to see the life drama worked out in front of them, I do believe," proclaimed drummer Mickey Hart in a 1976 radio interview.

Consistency is not the paramount virtue in this band. "If we go on the pat hand—what we know we can do —it gets stale real quick and we can't do it anymore," says Weir. "Interaction is what makes the Grateful Dead happen."

Interaction of a very special kind is the subject of *More than Human*, the 1953 science fiction novel in which author Theodore Sturgeon posited the concept of a human gestalt—the proverbial whole that is greater than the sum of its

17

OUTTAKE FROM A PHOTO SESSION FOR AN AD IN WHICH THE GRATEFUL DEAD MODELED CLOTHES FROM THE HAIGHT STREET BOUTIQUE MNASIDIKA. BACK COVER PHOTO IS THE ONE USED IN THE ADVERTISEMENT.

parts. The protagonist of the story was a being comprised of several individuals who didn't do particularly well on their own but found that their special qualities added up to something much greater than what they would have had had they all been whole, "normal" people.

This notion has been central to the Grateful Dead's explanation of itself from the start. Bob Weir has frequently referred to the Dead's modus operandi as "misfit power," and he once characterized the Grateful Dead as "a bunch of guys who would probably amount to neighborhood heroes but for the fact that we've fallen in with each other."

Phil Lesh had read *More than Human* by the time he joined the band that became the Grateful Dead. The book didn't exactly provide a blueprint for group consciousness, but it suggested to him that the possibility existed. Still, like the characters in the novel, the Grateful Dead didn't

see the extent of their collective potential at first. "We didn't declare it," said Lesh in 1983. "It declared us.

"Great bands have chemistry. Either they've played together for a long time, or the musicians are so great that despite being different, they can make great music together. When we first started, playing five-set shows six nights a week, we knew we could be a good band. But this went to some other level; the reality was so immediate that it couldn't be denied.

"At one point I just knew, and I assumed everybody else knew," Lesh continues. "I couldn't walk away from this—it was too *interesting*, fraught with meaning of greater breadth and scope and significance than I had ever imagined. I thought, We're on to something here. This is worth pursuing as far as it takes us.

"Acid helped, too," he adds.

LSD was the liberating flux that opened the players' minds to the potential for unconscious and/or superconscious communication. It was also the *raison d'etre* for the Acid Test, a do-it-yourselves, free-form happening/party thrown by novelist/social experimenter Ken Kesey's band of Merry Pranksters. LSD was the "unglue," and virtually any and every available bit of physical and mental matter provided the raw materials for the creation of nondenominational, overamped, unpoliced *fun*. "That was like someone saying, 'Okay, now we're going to go to warp speed,'" Lesh recalls. "And BOOM! Push the button and

"The Grateful Dead have proven that you can get there from here. It's just that there's no tickets available." —BILL KREUTZMANN

away we go!" It was the freest imaginable situation in which to let music develop along its own natural course rather than according to the usual rock band model.

As the house band at this awakening, not only did the Grateful Dead not have to play the popular songs of the day, they didn't necessarily have to play at all! So what they did (and by the way, they started doing it indecently soon after starting to play at all) was build a genuinely democratic, anarchic music that encompassed the many different styles favored by the five players.

Absent any rules or traditional leadership, each of these ambitious, talented, arrogant, un-polished, *game* cats did what he could and what made sense to him. And because they had a place to do it, they got good at it without ever having to worry much about how long the songs were, how weird their lyrics were, how accessible the sounds and melodies were. People dug this music and danced to it; what more did a band need to nurture a music? Declares Lesh, "We became the Grateful Dead at the Acid Test."

HERBIE GREENE

1
The Players

WHEN THERE WAS NO EAR TO HEAR

"History is what you remember, and if you don't think it's being revised all the time, you haven't paid enough attention to your own memory. When you remember something, you don't remember the thing itself—you just remember the last time you remembered it." —JOHN BARLOW

"It's still hard for me to have a clear mind thinking on it. But it's the truth even if it didn't happen."

—Ken Kesey, *One Flew Over the Cuckoo's Nest*

JERRY GARCIA

When I was fifteen I got a good old Danelectro guitar with a kind of coffin-shaped case, and I got a little teeny-weeny Fender amplifier. I was so happy with them. My stepfather tuned the guitar to this weird bogus tuning—or maybe he tuned it right and I evolved it to a wrong tuning.

I wanted to play like Chuck Berry more than anything else in the world. I learned some of the songs that were going around then, but I had no idea how to play, really. I worked out stuff that sounded good, figured out chords, and played along, but with absolutely no direction, in this silly open tuning that sounded good to my ear. I didn't know anybody who played guitar, and I was too arrogant to take lessons.

Then I met a guy in high school who showed me the right way to tune it and taught me four or five chords. I had to unlearn somewhere between six months and a year's worth of self-teaching. I really was a slow learner.

Later on I got interested in folk music—finger-style guitar playing—and then I devoted all my energy to five-string banjo for about three years. I came back to the guitar when we formed the band.

I didn't really get into the guitar with any kind of depth at all until the Grateful Dead started. Even then, it took a long time.

"Lost my boots in transit . . ."

Events in my life suggested to me that maybe it was going to be my responsibility to keep upping the ante. I was in an automobile accident in 1960 with four other guys. . . . ninety-plus miles an hour on a back road. We hit these dividers and went flying, I guess. All I know is that I was sitting in the car and there was this . . . disturbance . . . and the next thing I was in a field, far enough away from the car that I couldn't see it.

The car was like a crumpled cigarette pack . . . and inside it were my shoes! I'd been thrown out of my shoes and through the windshield. . . .

One guy did die, the most gifted in our little group. It was like losing the golden boy, the person who had the most to offer. For me it was crushing, but I had a feeling that my life had been spared to *do* something . . . to not take any bullshit, to either go whole hog or not at all. . . . That's the only way to do it. You keep parlaying what you've got, because the whole thing is a dream when you come right down to it. The worst thing that can happen is you end up back where you were, and back where we were is something we all can handle. So since you're out there in dreamland to begin with, the thing to do is keep going for it.

That was where my life began. Before then I was always living at less than capacity. That event was the slingshot for the rest of my life. It was my second chance; then I got serious.

22

MICHAEL DOBO

HERBIE GREENE

BOB WEIR

I wanted to play and sing, and the guitar was portable. You could accompany yourself without having to cart a piano around, and that made it impossibly seductive.

I liked the Everly Brothers, the Kingston Trio, Joan Baez, and Chuck Berry a lot. When I first heard the Kingston Trio, here were three guys who could make a lot of music all by themselves. I quickly dumped them as heroes as soon as I heard Joan Baez all by herself playing guitar and doing real well.

From there I started finding out about others, like Reverend Gary Davis, Doc Watson, and Robert Johnson. I learned a lot about the range of what's available in American folk music; I was fairly well-grounded in that by the time I got into rock and roll.

I spent my last year of school learning the guitar. Didn't attend a single class. I was going to a really loose, progressive school at the time, and they figured if that's what I was looking for in an education that's what I'd get. By God, I got it—and I'm relatively happy that I did.

How'd you manage to get thrown out of so many schools?

[*Shrugs*] Fun, fun, fun. I didn't get in fights or anything like that—I was just a disciplinary problem, I guess what you'd call a yahoo. I got decent grades; I couldn't read, so I learned how to listen fast and bullshit even faster.

In high school I had a group called the Uncalled Four. It wasn't much of a band—we performed, I think, once, at the Tangent in Palo Alto. I met Garcia briefly backstage that night. He was playing with the Black Mountain Boys. I didn't really meet him on concrete terms until a few months later, on New Year's Eve.

23

LINDA McCARTNEY

"FOR THE LONGEST TIME, PEOPLE MISTOOK WEIR FOR A GIRL."—JERRY GARCIA

BARON WOLMAN

BOB WEIR AT HIS MILL VALLEY HOME, 1972

BILL KREUTZMANN

In grade school orchestras they don't have drum sets—you play the bass drum, snare drum, cymbals, etc. If you don't have a drum of your own and you can't afford a snare drum, they give you the school's bass drum to play. That's what I got in the sixth grade when I started, but by around the second class session the teacher said, "Bill, you have to leave, because you can't keep a beat." It totally crushed me. I was *so* hurt. I'll never forget it. . . . To turn off a kid at that age is criminal.

Because of that incident, I left music for a while. Yet it was *that* kind of thing that made me real gutsy. I said to myself, Am I going to let this teacher tell me I can't be a drummer? Hell, no!

My dad . . . rented me a snare drum. That Saturday afternoon I went over to another kid's house—he had a bass, and this other kid had a guitar—and the three of us played. And we probably played like shit!

There were some local cronies hanging out—this was seventh or eighth grade—and I looked around the room and they were all smiling and digging it. That's when I first flashed, Wow! Music really does make people happy. And I sure wanted to get into something that makes people feel good.

I practiced in the garage, endlessly. Once a neighbor beat on the wall with a bat—out of time and everything. I'd stop, it'd stop; I'd begin, he'd hit some more. My dad told him, "Leave my son alone!" and "You're pounding on *my* garage!" He was totally supportive.

I used to listen to James Brown's drummer and also a lot of Motown stuff. And jazz, too—Joe Morello, Elvin Jones . . . I try to use what I know about different styles in our music to make it more interesting.

25

THEY WERE STILL THE WARLOCKS WHEN THIS PICTURE OF KREUTZMANN WAS TAKEN.

HERBIE GREENE

HERBIE GREENE

PHIL LESH IN 1967

TOM COPI

PHIL LESH

I got into popular music backwards: Until I was sixteen or seventeen my entire input was classical. Then I got into jazz, which led to the blues, which led me to rock and roll.

I was in my room one Sunday when I was very young, and the Philharmonic was playing on the radio. My grandmother discovered me on the floor with my ear to the wall, listening to the music. Come next Sunday, a few minutes before the broadcast, she asked me if I'd like to come and listen with her.

The program was Brahms' First, conducted by Bruno Walter. The introduction came on like the wrath of God! As soon as I heard that, I just *knew.*

When I was in the third grade I brought home a violin. Listening to someone learning the violin is worse than listening to seventeen cats howling in unison, but my parents were patient. I played second violin in orchestras, but it really wasn't my instrument.

I took up the trumpet at fourteen, and for some reason I was something of a prodigy. Within a year I was able to play concert band lead parts, and by the time I finished my sophomore year, I was in the second chair.

Then my parents did me the greatest favor anybody could have done: They moved to Berkeley so I could go to Berkeley High, where they had harmony and theory courses—the stuff I really wanted.

I got into jazz because of the later big bands, the nineteen-piece outfits of the late forties and early fifties. The first time I heard Coltrane I was incensed—"How dare the guy play like that!" Maybe it was the tone—Coltrane's tone in the late fifties was *really* abrasive. But I finally got over whatever it was.

I didn't like Miles Davis at first, either. His tone in the late fifties was breathy, not the kind of trumpet tone I'd been taught was hip. It was hard to accept that there was more than one way to do anything, especially play an instrument.

I went to the College of San Mateo [CSM] and joined their jazz band—five trumpets, five saxophones, five trombones, and four rhythm instruments. Playing in a unit like that knocks your socks off; when they're swinging together, not even a symphony orchestra is quite like it.

That was one of the first times I submerged my craving to play the top part. That was a *big flash*, thinking, It's just as cool to do this as be the soloist.

Eventually the one guy ahead of me left school, and I had to take over. I didn't do as good a job as he did, *so I gave up the trumpet!*

While I was in the jazz band, though, I wrote my first two pieces. I picked up orchestration pretty much on my own; if you sit in a symphony orchestra or a band, you can get a very good idea of what it's all about. This was direct creation: composition, laying it down on paper. It was more or less mainstream stuff; I just wanted to see what would happen if I wrote it down and they played it.

By this time I'd been turned on—to pot and Kerouac and Allen Ginsberg. I loved *Howl* so much I started to set it to music.

I had a job in the library at CSM, listening to the new records that came in and making sure there weren't any pops or scratches on them.

That was when I first heard of electronic music, music that could be made out of its most minute components and stored on tape and controlled by the composer without having to go through a performer!

I finally got to UC Berkeley, and I found that it was for musicologists—people who study *about* music. I met Tom Constanten [TC], who later played in the Grateful Dead, when we were registering in the music department.

◆   ◆   ◆

TC: I was discussing music with this person, who turned out to be Phil Lesh, and a woman called Margie Panovsky. . . . I made a pontifical statement, as seventeen-year-olds are wont to make, that perhaps music stopped being created in 1450 but it started again in 1950—referring specifically to the *avant-gardists* with whom my adolescent mind was so captivated.

Phil immediately extended his hand to me and we shook most heartily.

LESH: Here was somebody I could talk to! He became my roommate, and we spent more time together than either one of us did in class. Musical Analysis was pretty interesting, but we spent half a semester on one Bach fugue. And I got a C in it to boot. I became pretty disillusioned. I quit school after that, but I didn't tell my parents for weeks.

TC: . . . We laid the cornerstone for a mutual admiration society for one another's work that has remained throughout the years. Phil introduced me to his people, among whom was a folk singer called Jerry Garcia. . . .

LESH: Luciano Berio, one of the composers of the time whose music seemed *musical*, came to Mills College [in nearby Oakland] to teach. TC went right over there with his pieces; I was chicken. This was graduate level, and neither of us had had a full semester of college. But Berio invited TC to join the class, and when he asked if he could bring his roommate along, Berio said, "Okay, have him bring something he's written."

Those six months were an intense experience. Berio didn't teach—it just *radiated* from him. The guy was—and still is—a magician. I love him.

27

MICKEY HART

My mother and father were both rudimental drummers, involved in the drum corps scene on the East Coast in the thirties and forties. My mother taught me the rudiments.

Neighbors would come to the door to complain, but my mother would say, "He's going to be a drummer!" . . . Supportive parents are so very important. My advice to a young drummer is, "Man, get good parents!"

Years ago, when I was starting to play drums, I came into a new high school as a freshman. I had my sticks, I knew the rudiments, and I wanted to be in the band. Mr. Jones [Arthur Jones, the band teacher at Lawrence High School on Long Island] said, "Mickey, there are twenty-eight drummers in the band. I don't know what I can do. Play for me."

So I played him a couple ratta-tats. Had he said no, I might have . . . given up drumming, at least. He said, "Okay, you can be in Band Two," and he put a strap on me and I pulled the bass drum in the band. Finally worked my way up through the cymbals, the tenor drum line, and finally snare.

I started to play rock and roll in small clubs on the weekends. I thought the first trio I had was a rock and roll band—I was playing the drums, and we had an accordion and a valve trombone! Then we got into guitars, but we still didn't know what we were doing.

I went into the Air Force, because they have the best rudimental drummers in the world and I figured that was the only way to get next to drummers of that caliber. I spent a lot of time playing—in clubs at night and in marching bands during the day.

When I came out, I started a drum store on the [San Francisco] Peninsula.

I met Kreutzmann at the Fillmore when Count Basie was playing. I was hangin' out with his drummer, Sonny Payne. We were good friends. I loved Basie, and I featured myself as a big-band drummer then.

Kreutzmann and I met that night. I think someone pointed him out to me. . . . I knew

HERBIE GREENE

about the Grateful Dead. We started talking about drums, and we went out that night with a bottle of Scotch and went around playing on cars. We weren't beatin' 'em up or anything—we were trying to make music.

I had seen Grace Slick, but I had never really seen Janis. Kreutzmann said, "You want to see fire and ice? That's Janis and Grace." So we went to see Janis at the Matrix, and we took Sonny Payne with us. James Gurley picked up his guitar and he raped it. I'd never seen anything like it. It was magnificent, the best solo I'd ever heard. That amplifier was just pulsing on the floor. Sonny couldn't stand it, because it was too loud. I said, "I'm not going anywhere. This is great!" Sonny got a headache and walked out of my life that night.

Kreutzmann told me about the Dead, and I went to see them at the Straight Theater. The place was so big and the PA was so monstrous that everything was getting washed out. All you could hear was the bass and Jerry—you couldn't hear any vocals, really, and you couldn't hear Kreutzmann. It was magnificent, though.

The feeling was incredible. I couldn't tell where they were going; it was so unusual. I thought I really would like to play with this band.

29

I thought this would be an incredible challenge. I thought it had great spiritual content. Whatever hit me at that moment wasn't within the realm of logic or understanding—it felt like some kind of force field from another planet, some incredible energy that was driving the band and pulling you in at the same time. This was what music should be like. It was very special—not your normal entertainment fare. It was prayerlike music; it wasn't music that was going into the music business.

Kreutzmann asked me to play in the second set . . . and we really did play "Alligator" for two hours.

That night was really inspired. It had to be, in order for me to play with the band forever.

Not everybody would have been attracted to that music——

Of course not! Nor would just anybody have wanted to *do* it. That's why I'm in the Grateful Dead and they're not. It's that simple: I think there's a calling for it. There was no way you could academically, technically, or mathematically keep up with the Grateful Dead; it would be impossible. And we didn't know as much then as we do now, so it had to have come from another place. It was magic.

. . . We've got transformation going here. We don't have a popular recording group. That's what the trappings may look like in some respects, but that ain't what we have.

It is a musical organization, but we're not necessarily involved exclusively, or even primarily, in music.

30

BRUCE POLONSKY

DAVID GANS

YES, THAT'S MICKEY HART WITH HIS HEAD SHAVED. YOU'LL HAVE TO ASK *HIM* WHY HE DID IT—IT WAS ALL WE COULD DO TO GET HIM TO AGREE TO LET US PRINT THE PICTURE.

ED PERLSTEIN

BRENT MYDLAND

I joined my first band when I was in high school in Concord [California]. I don't know if you'd call it a rock and roll band. I don't know whether you'd qualify it as a *band*—I got together with some friends and started playing around. We had a drummer, sort of, a bass player, sort of, and a guitar player, sort of. It was pretty much whoever wanted to play at the time. We never really made over ten bucks a head.

In the seventies I started listening to stuff like Herbie Hancock and Jimmy Smith, and I got out of trying to write and got into jamming and playing in club bands. I started getting back into rock and roll around '74.

I turned pro in '75; I went to LA with the intention of breaking into the biz. I worked with Batdorf and Rodney for a while, after the last of their three albums was made. We made one single, but not much came of it.

Then [guitarists] Greg Collier, John Batdorf, and I got a band together called Silver. We made an album for Arista and a semi-hit called "Wham-Bam"—"We got a wham bam shang-a-lang and a sha la la la la la la thing." It was embarrassing. It was written by somebody outside the band. We got dropped by Arista a year later.

In Silver I was writing and singing lead as well as playing keyboards, and I could express my own ideas. I wanted to get into another band; I kicked around down there for a while, but I never came up with anything I was satisfied with. I did some session work, just enough to pick up some spare bucks, and then I moved back to Northern California. There was work in LA, but I got into a slump; I came back north [in 1978] because I knew more musicians personally and thought maybe I could get something together.

Within a couple of weeks of moving back here I got a call from John Mauceri. Bob Weir had hired him for a tour [after the release of *Heaven Help the Fool* in January 1978], and they needed a keyboard player.

My audition for Weir was just "come and play with us and see what happens"—which was pretty much the way it was when I auditioned for the Dead.

DAVID GANS

BRENT MYDLAND, 1984

HERBIE GREENE

BRENT MYDLAND, 1980

2
The Band

FOR THIS IS ALL A DREAM WE DREAMED

"It's that impish facet of the human spirit, that no matter how good you've got it, you think it should be better—not just for you, but for everybody. That's what drove a bunch of relatively well-off suburban kids to band together to make music that was in some way expressive of a fairly critical view of the social structure that spawned them. Not because they were starving, but because they felt it could be better." —BOB WEIR

GARCIA: We were a social configuration of some kind before we were a band. Our roots are in that strictly good-time thing, basic hippies, without any kind of motive or purpose. It's one of the things that's given us a sort of community strength.

The Grateful Dead just kind of grew out of the side of this social scene. There was no logic to it at all.

I met Phil at the old Palo Alto Peace Center, which was where the sons and daughters of the Stanford professors would hang out and discuss things. And we, the opportunist wolf pack, the beatnik hordes, would be there preying on their young minds and their refrigerators. . . .

Phil and I were in two different worlds musically, but we always got along really good. He had a girlfriend in Palo Alto, and when he was around he'd hang out at St. Michael's Alley, which was where I and Hunter and various other people were hanging out. You could sit over a cup of coffee all night, in the course of some apocalyptic conversation. . . .

"Time there was and plenty . . ."

LESH: I was the engineer for the "Midnight Special" [a folk music program on Berkeley's KPFA, hosted by Gert Chiarito]. Jerry was at this party in Palo Alto, singing and playing his guitar. I had found things to enjoy in that kind of music, and I was impressed by somebody who could sing and play. . . .

I said, "Hey, Jerry, if we could make a tape of you playing and singing, would you mind if I took it to Gert and played it for her?"

He rode with me back to Berkeley to get the tape recorder—this was when we had *all the time in the universe*—and he played and sang five or six songs. I didn't know how good he was, I just knew I liked him.

I played the tape for Gert and asked her if he was good enough to play on the "Midnight Special." She said, "This guy could have a show all to himself." So they did an hour show called "Long Black Veil," because that was one of the songs he

TOM COPI

BOB WEIR, 1967

34

was doing at the time. Jerry played and sang, and he rapped with Gert.

After that he was almost a regular. And he started bringing his buddies up from Palo Alto.

"Nothin' else shakin'
So you might just as well"

WEIR: On New Year's Eve of 1963, a friend of mine and I were wandering the back streets of Palo Alto. We were way too young to get into any of the hot clubs. We'd worked it out so we could get into one folk club, but there was nothing happening that night—or at least not yet.

So we were walking the back streets of Palo Alto, just talking things over. We walked by the back of this music store that we used to frequent—Dana Morgan Music—and we heard banjo music. This seemed strange to us, because

it was New Year's Eve, so we knocked on the door.

It was Garcia. I didn't know him at the time, but we recognized him from the numerous bands he was in. He was *the* local hot banjo player. He was in there waiting for his students to show up, absolutely unmindful of the fact that it was New Year's Eve and absolutely none of them were coming. We acquainted him with that information, and we started talking.

Garcia had been playing for a few hours, and I could tell he was hot to play with somebody. We knew he had the key to the front of the shop, so we talked him into breaking in, and we grabbed a couple of the guitars we'd always wanted to play.

We had a good time playing and singing and kicking stuff around all night, and by the end of the evening—I don't know what time it was—we decided we probably had enough second-rate talent there to throw together a jug band, which was a popular trend in folk music at the time. We called a rehearsal for a few days from then. I knew a guy or two, Garcia knew several guys, and we'd sort it out when we got there.

GARCIA: Jug band is essentially country music, in that it's rural. It was mostly a result of musicians not having enough money to buy fancy instruments. So they bought kazoos and used whatever was around.

WEIR: I really couldn't play guitar at all, so I got relegated to jug and washtub bass—which I also couldn't play at all, but they figured if anybody had to start from scratch it probably ought to be me.

The next day I got a washtub and a broom handle and a piece of string and a bunch of

TOM SNYDER: *Did you ever think when you were starting that it would evolve into this mystique that's come to surround the group?*

BOB WEIR: *We didn't think when we were starting . . .*

BOB SEIDEMANN

A ROW OF BRAND-NEW, PASTEL-COLORED TRACT HOUSES IN DALY CITY, JUST SOUTH OF SAN FRANCISCO. ALONG WITH THE FIVE BAND MEMBERS, THE PHOTOGRAPHER BROUGHT "FIVE HIPPIES TO SHINE MIRRORS IN THEIR FACES" TO CREATE THIS EFFECT. THE COPS ARRIVED AND BROKE IT UP A FEW MINUTES LATER.

different kinds of jugs and showed up at the next rehearsal. God knows how, but I figured out how to play them all. I could make notes happen with a washtub bass . . . and the jug, too.

We listened to a bunch of old jug band records that various guys had rounded up, and then we started working on the songs, country blues and standard jug band stuff like "Stealin' " and "Minglewood Blues," and Jesse Fuller tunes like "Beat It on Down the Line" and "Monkey and the Engineer."

GARCIA: Our jug band was complete and total anarchy. Just lots and lots of people in it, and Pigpen [singer Ron McKernan] and Bob and I were more or less the ringleaders. We'd work out various kinds of musically funny material. It was like a musical vacation to get on stage and have a good time.

WEIR: We became really popular around the mid-Peninsula area—had work just about every weekend. We were called Mother McCree's Uptown Jug Champions.

All the time we were first getting started, we were really happy playing jug band music. And we were getting real good at it. But after we got to be pretty tight, we started wondering what we were going to do. People started quitting the band, to go away to school or this or that, and at one point Garcia left on a tour of the South to study bluegrass music. By the time he got back a couple of months later, we didn't know what we were going to do. Re-forming the jug band wasn't it.

About that time the Beatles started to become popular. Garcia had been playing in rock and roll bands all along—guitar and bass, whatever was required of him—to bolster his income. We started kicking around the idea of maybe firing up electric guitars and playing some blues, Chicago style or Jimmy Reed style or whatever.

HERBIE GREENE

HERBIE GREENE

36

GARCIA: Pigpen had been pestering me for a while to start up an electric blues band. That was his trip . . . because in the jug band scene we used to do blues numbers, like Jimmy Reed tunes.

WEIR: Finally, through the shop, we got Billy [Kreutzmann] involved. He was working in various bands, and I think he was working at a wig shop or something like that—whatever genuine paying gig he could get. He was married at the time I met him.

I was lucky enough to get a job teaching beginning and intermediate students on the guitar. Pigpen worked at the music store so he couldn't hang out with musicians, but basically he didn't want to work any more than he absolutely had to. Playing was different—that wasn't like working, for Pig.

The son of the owner of the shop [Dana Morgan, Jr.] wanted to be the bass player, and suddenly we had a band—especially since the son of the owner of the shop could supply the instruments.

GARCIA: Kreutzmann was not a guy I knew socially. He was not a part of our scene. I got hold of him because I knew he was a player. I don't think I would have gotten to know him in a regular life, in a way, because he's a very different kind of person. It's been interesting getting to know him.

KREUTZMANN: I wasn't part of the jug band . . .

never saw them play. I had played more rock than any of those guys.

We started practicing at Dana Morgan Music, in a small room crammed with equipment. Pigpen was the lead singer on all the songs. They didn't know much about rock music, and it was pretty much the beginning for me, too, even though I'd been playing in rock bands for a little while.

WEIR: Along about New Year's Eve of the next year, we had gone from being a jug band to being a serious, hard-working rock and roll band. Called ourselves the Warlocks. We played about six months that way, and then the son of the owner of the store couldn't make our rehearsal schedule—not to mention our gig schedule—and had to drop out.

GARCIA: It was obvious to me: "Right on, Phil would love this!" It just seemed like that kind of thing. I knew he could do it—I didn't even have to think about that. But he was a *friend*; I didn't call him as a stranger, or even as a guy I knew that played.

"It may require a change
That hasn't come before . . ."

LESH: I hated rock and roll music. I thought, What can you do with three chords? I hated the Beatles at first, and then I went to see *A Hard*

Day's Night. I was the only guy in a theater full of screamin' chicks. I thought, There's got to be something to this! And then I started to grow my hair long.

I was completely divorced from music as a participant, but I was listening to everything I could suck up. By that time I was open enough to accept Dylan. I was working for the post office when *Bringing It All Back Home* came out. You weren't supposed to do this, but I had a little radio in the truck with me. "Subterranean Homesick Blues" came on, and I said, "Fuck me, that's Bob Dylan! On the AM radio!" I forgot about my route, pulled over, and listened. I couldn't believe it—and apparently they couldn't believe it at KFRC, either, because they played it about three times an hour that whole day.

I ran into Garcia at a party in Palo Alto. I'd been listening to the Beatles, the Rolling Stones. . . . Jerry and I were raving, and at some point I mentioned that I might like to get into playing some electric instrument—maybe bass guitar or something like that. It was a stoned moment, and I didn't think anything more about it.

WEIR: We were talking about the problem of Dana Morgan not being able to make the rehearsals and gigs, and Garcia said he knew a guy who was a great musician, who wrote music and played trumpet and was particularly crazy and fun to be with. He said, "He doesn't play the bass, but if we give him a couple of weeks I'm sure he could."

LESH: My friends and I took acid and went to see Garcia's band play at Magoo's Pizza Parlor. We came boppin' in there, and Pigpen ate my mind with the harp, singing the blues. They wouldn't let you dance, but I did anyway. We were so stoned!

During the break Jerry took me off to a table and told me their bass player couldn't handle the schedule and asked me if I'd like to play in the band. It excited the shit out of me because it was—at last!—something to do. It was so ironic, because I'd just about quit music entirely. The flash was, "You mean I can get paid for having fun?"

I said, "By God, I'll give it a try."

"You got to play your hand
some time
The cards ain't worth a dime
If you don't lay 'em down"

WEIR: I met Phil at Magoo's one night, and the next week he was in the band. We already had a following at this point, so we just added him and went on working.

It was obvious to me as a musician that certain fundamentals had to be observed—deal with the bass drum, play the root of certain chords—but I figured out pretty quickly that a whole bunch of that could be disposed of. I *could* play off-beat to the bass-drum, put the seventh or even the ninth in the bass, and it would still make sense.

My first gig was across the Bay in Hayward. We had an oral deal for two or three nights, and the first night was my first night in the band. There was nobody there—I guess the guy had expected us to draw automatically or something.

We took all our equipment home with us that night because they wouldn't guarantee any security for it, and when we came back the next night there was a saxophone, accordion, and guitar trio playing. Either we were so bad—which was possible—or the club owner was just desperate, but we'd been replaced. And I don't think we ever got paid for the first night.

"It could be an illusion
But I might as well try"

LESH: The decision to change the name meant we were getting serious, because we couldn't make a record if some other band had the same name as us.

I told the boys I was in a record store, thumbing through 45s, and I'd seen a record with the name the Warlocks on it. I've often wondered whether I hallucinated it, because I never saw the record again and I never heard a word about any band called the Warlocks.

GARCIA: We were trying to think up names, and for about two or three weeks we went on the usual thing of coming up with thousands and thousands of very funny names, none of which

37

we could use—like Vitamin E and the Vivisectionists——

WEIR: Here and Now and the Reality Sandwich . . .

GARCIA: We were standing around in utter desperation at Phil's house in Palo Alto. There was a huge dictionary, big monolithic thing, and I just opened it up. There in huge black letters was "The Grateful Dead." It . . . just cancelled my mind out.

We decided to have it, but it was funny. . . . One of the things about the name, right from the beginning, was that it had a lot of power. It was kind of creepy. People resisted it at first. They didn't want us to be the Grateful Dead—it was too weird. But . . . I don't think the connotation is nearly as creepy as it used to be, though sometimes the *power* is very evident.

LESH: At first I thought, Okay, we'll make it five years and then take the money and run. It

38

HERBIE GREENE

didn't work out like that—there was more to it than just making money and getting laid all the time.

It wasn't just . . . fun.

LESH: No. It turned out to be life. My nervousness over maybe not being able to play the bass with any degree of musicality got blown away in the first rehearsal. We all learned how to play together, and that's why we play well together.

I remember saying to the guys, "You know, this could be art!" And they laughed, because they knew already.

". . . I broke away and found that my new world had different values from my old one and in the new I was valuable. I was wanted, I belonged."

—Theodore Sturgeon,
More than Human

JERILYN BRANDELIUS COLLECTION

"I WASN'T INTO THE ETHNOLOGY OF THE CLOTHES—I WAS INTO THE COLORS. I THOUGHT THIS LOOKED LIKE MARIJUANA, SO I GOT IT."—PHIL LESH

CHAPTER

3
Acid Test

SHALL WE GO, YOU AND I, WHILE WE CAN?

"We were lucky to have a little moment in history when LSD was still legal and we could experiment with drugs like we were experimenting with music." —JERRY GARCIA

"The bus come by and I got on
That's when it all began"

LSD had been part of the Grateful Dead's scene since before there was a Grateful Dead. Robert Hunter was one of the bright young guinea pigs (writer Ken Kesey was another) who was given acid, mescaline, psilocybin, and other substances in a laboratory at Stanford University so that government scientists could observe their behavior.

The fun those people had in those little rooms inspired them to conduct a few experiments of their own, in much less clinical surroundings. "We were playing around in this house," Garcia recalled. "We had a couple of Day-Glow super balls, and we bounced them around and we were just reading comic books, doodling, strumming guitars, just doing stuff. . . . All of a sudden you remember that you are free to *play*! We were rediscovering the world and playing with all these wonderful things."

Acid showed the Warlocks that playing "short, fast stuff" in bars and night clubs wasn't going to

remain appropriate much longer. "We began to see that vision of a truly fantastic thing." And Ken Kesey's Merry Pranksters soon provided a context in which to pursue it.

♦　　♦　　♦

WEIR: One day the idea was there: "Why don't we have a big party? You guys bring your instruments and play, and us Pranksters will set up all our tape recorders and stuff, and we'll all get stoned." And that was the first Acid Test.

The idea was formless. There was nothing going *on*—we'd just go up there and make something of it.

GARCIA: The Pranksters were having these parties at their place in La Honda, and they wanted to move the parties out into the world a little bit and just see what happens.

The first one was in San Jose, right after the Stones concert, the same night [December 4, 1965]. We went there and played, but our equipment damn near filled the room, and we were real loud . . . there were hundreds and hundreds of people swarming around this guy's house.

After that we had a meeting, and we decided to keep on doing it. But having it in somebody's house didn't make it, so the idea was . . . to move it to a different location each time.

The Acid Test was the prototype for the whole Grateful Dead trip.

LESH: The Acid Tests were the only place our music ever had a real sense of proportion to an event.

GARCIA: It wasn't a gig, it was the Acid Test. Anything was okay. Thousands of people, all helplessly stoned, finding themselves in a room full of other people, none of whom any of them were afraid of. It was magic—far out, beautiful magic.

We had no reputation, and nobody was paying to see us or anything like that. We weren't the headliners, the *event* was. Anything that happened was part of it, so everybody who came there was free to enjoy the show or to *be* the show if they felt like it.

There was always the option to *not* play. Sometimes we'd play for five minutes and then freak out—"*I can't play anymore! It's too weird!*"—for an hour or two, then filter back to the instruments and play for hours.

The freedom was what I loved about it. When you're high, you might want to play for five hours, but sometimes you might want to stick your head in a bucket of water, or have some jello or something.

"There was a happy and fearless communion, fearlessly shared . . . reciprocal thought and mutual achievement."

—Theodore Sturgeon,
More than Human

WEIR: Right away we dropped completely out of the straight music scene and just played the Tests for six months: San Jose, Palo Alto, Muir Beach, Portland, the Trips Festival . . . and then [in February 1966] LA.

GARCIA: It cost a buck, and everybody paid it—the musicians, the electricians, the guy that collected the tickets—and if there was only one buck we'd all pay it over and over again. It cost you a buck and you stayed there all night.

"There was Cowboy Neal
At the wheel
Of a bus to Never Ever Land"

One of the people responsible for joining the Grateful Dead and Prankster scenes was Neal Cassady, a speed merchant in more ways than one. In this realm where coincidence has always been more than coincidentally efficacious, he may well have known that he was more than just the pot connection when he sold Bobby Weir the lid he brought to the party on the night Garcia introduced him to Phil Lesh—the same night Lesh, in a "stoned moment," mentioned to Garcia that he might want to play some electric music.

LESH: I met him in 1963, when he was selling methedrine in little vials, and pot. He was the only person I ever knew who resembled what they used to call a saint, someone who could be a role model for the real spiritual life. It may seem incongruous——

The sacred and the profane——

HERBIE GREENE

MOUNTAIN GIRL (NEE CAROLYN ADAMS) STAYED WITH THE GRATEFUL DEAD—AND WITH GARCIA—WHEN THE ACID TESTS ENDED.

SAN FRANCISCO, 1966

HERBIE GREENE

LESH: Yeah. He was a saint for us; he was a saint for me. He showed by example how to live in the weirdest possible way. He inspired weirdness, among many other things.

GARCIA: Neal represented how far you could go in the individual way. . . . I had been an art student and was wavering between one man/one work and being involved in something in which I wasn't the only contributing factor. I decided to go with what was dynamic and ongoing and didn't necessarily stay one way.

LESH: It wasn't so much the energy he represented—it was the articulation of that energy into *meaning*.

It was like he had a field around him that reached far away from him and made things happen before he got there physically. One time I was driving up the Bayshore Freeway toward San Francisco with a friend, and traffic slowed to a crawl around Candlestick Park because there was a Giants game.

Everything was inching along at about three miles an hour, and it looked like there was no room for anything—but suddenly there was a commotion behind us, and it was a car coming *through the traffic!* Somehow the cars were getting out of the way in front of it, like the shock wave in front of a rocket.

The guy in the car with me knew Neal, too. I didn't even want to dare to think it, but I looked at him, and just then the car went by, and it *was* Neal—car full of people, feelin' up a chick in the back, drivin' with one hand, playin' the radio, going through this traffic. Everybody else was doing three miles an hour, and Neal was doing twenty. He knew they'd get out of his way, just like he always knew whether or not there was a car around the corner when he went around it on the wrong side of the street with two wheels up on the sidewalk.

WEIR: Neal used to be able to drive through downtown San Francisco at rush hour at around fifty-five miles an hour, never stopping for a stoplight or a stop sign or anything like that. Nobody could figure out how he could do it. He was an amazing man.

GARCIA: People would dismiss him as crazy, but in my mind he was the complete communicator. He always had a stream going, and you could jump right in and he'd always take into account that you were there.

LESH: It wasn't just his rap, which was incredibly funny, and it wasn't just how interesting he was. When Neal was rapping, not only was he talking to everybody in the car at once—four or

43

NEAL CASSADY

HERBIE GREENE

five people—but he was also driving the car and playing what we used to call "Radio I Ching": Every time he hit the button, whatever came out of the radio made sense with what he was saying or was otherwise complementary to what was going on.

There was nothing facile about him. Neal was always full on, and there was never any bullshit. He had the least bullshit coming out of him of anybody I've ever seen.

Even in my wildest dreams I don't believe that everybody's supposed to live like that, but I'd say he defined the cultural phenomenon that started in the fifties and is still reverberating now. He just personified it. He was like a great artist whose art form was his life.

Was his writing any good?

LESH: I've only read this thing called *The First Third,* and it's pale compared to his talkin'. Like a Grateful Dead record.

◆   ◆   ◆

The Acid Tests brought the Grateful Dead into contact with another successful exemplar of Misfit Power: Owsley Stanley, also known as Bear, a dropout many times over who learned a lot about a lot of things along the way.

Owsley gained world renown as the maker of the best acid you could get—better even than the Swiss pharmaceutical stuff the U.S. government used. "The Bear really was responsible for turning *millions* of people on to acid," said Lesh in 1984.

He showed up at the Muir Beach Acid Test in December of 1965. "Bear heard that there were musicians getting together and playing stoned on acid, and he had to find out what was going on," Lesh recalls. "He came to meet us, but I knew him already! I'd been eating his acid for a year.

"For him, the Acid Test was suspicions confirmed: The gestalt does work."

"Who can stop what must
arrive now?
Something new is waiting to
be born"

LESH: In 1965, none of this was illegal. We thought we were really onto something—not just for ourselves, but politically, too, let's face it. We had some big ideas in the back of our heads. Nobody really talked about it, but we thought we could change the world. We'd play the music and show 'em how it can be done, and if we had to dose a few of 'em . . .

TROUPER'S HALL, LOS ANGELES, MARCH 1966

" 'Satisfaction' just came up one night . . . one of those little clouds of madness that drifted across the stage. We do it every now and then, usually when I'm feeling pretty ringy. We have never done that one remotely the same way twice, and obviously we've never, ever rehearsed it. There are a number of songs that we've never rehearsed, but 'Satisfaction' is one of the songs that rehearsal would ruin." —BOB WEIR

When we went to LA to do the Watts Acid Test, Garcia left his yellow four-door Corvair in a gas station in Palo Alto—with Weir's clothes in the trunk—and never saw it again. He had a ride to LA, and I got on a jet plane for the first time in my life and flew down with Bear. It was a red-eye flight, and we were the only two people in the back of a 707.

We got a big pink three-story house on the edge of Watts in January of 1966. That's when Bear started paying the bills. He was still paying the bills when we moved back up north, and by the time we moved into San Francisco in September, he had spent around $50,000—in *1966* dollars.

So that was nine months during which the Grateful Dead didn't have to make musical compromises to get work.

LESH: Right. We were able to be the Grateful Dead, and if we could get gigs, that was good. But at least we knew we'd have meat and milk and a roof over our heads.

Bear was our patron in the finest sense of the word. He didn't send us a check every month, he lived with us. He paid the bills and bought us time and space—well, he didn't buy it for us, we all bought it together. Bear will be the first to tell you that. And he never thought once about the money.

By the time the Acid Tests ended, we had struck up a bargain. He would build a sound system for us, and we'd play the music. It was the next step in keeping the game moving.

Was doing sound his way of joining the band?

LESH: He probably thought he could sway us this way or that, and he could. We were open. But it was never like Bear was writing our script for us.

Everything we do today is an offshoot of his ideas, which he developed through conversations with us. He knew enough about acoustics, but he had to understand what musicians wanted.

◆ ◆ ◆

GARCIA: The Acid Tests stopped because LSD became illegal. But if that could have kept on going, I'd still be doing it. It was tremendously fun and good and entertaining—what life should be, really.

LESH: After that, it was . . . real gigs, for money.

If the Acid Tests hadn't happened, we might have been just another band. But you can also say that without the Grateful Dead the Acid Tests

ROCK SCULLY AND TANGERINE

HERBIE GREENE

45

INSIDE 710 ASHBURY, 1966

GENE ANTHONY

46

wouldn't have happened in the same way. Or maybe we would have ended up with our own version of it sooner or later; that's what we were all into.

That was the real *baptismo del fuego*. When you're up there and your *face* is falling off and you've still got to play and you do this over and over again, spilling your guts in front of thousands of people . . . you develop a certain *flip* attitude, even toward performing. You begin to believe that you could go out there naked and nobody'd notice, as long as you played loud enough.

KREUTZMANN: It wasn't hard to play on acid at the Acid Tests [*laughs*]. I didn't know hard from easy at the Tests.

LSD is just a tool, anyway. You don't outgrow it, you learn what it has to teach you and grow from it. And it's not the only basis of the music— but it's one hell of a door to go through.

GARCIA: How gray life would be without psychedelics.

"It trembled and exploded
Left a bus stop in its place"

ROCK SCULLY [former Grateful Dead manager]: I, unfortunately, was promoting a show at California Hall the same night Kesey was doing an Acid Test at the Fillmore. Not wanting to get wiped out, I devised a plan with Kesey and some buses: If you bought a ticket to the Acid Test you could come to our show, and vice versa. The buses ran back and forth every twenty minutes.

That was the second time I saw the Grateful Dead. I split my own show, hopped on the bus, and went to see the Dead. As a matter of fact, once I left California Hall, I didn't go back, because when I got to the Fillmore the Dead were raisin' the roof. I fell in love with that band.

One of the most fascinating things about the Rolling Stones was those early photos. Boy, did they look ugly! There was a mystique about those ugly guys making that incredible music. And the Dead were even uglier than the Rolling Stones!

I said to myself, These guys will never make it commercially. The Dead didn't care what they looked like—they had Pigpen! They were *baaaad*-looking, and they *played*—heavy-duty rock and roll. They played a lot of the stuff that was making the Stones so popular, like "Little Red Rooster" and all that nitty-gritty blues . . .

BILL GRAHAM: The Dead and the Airplane and Quicksilver . . . we were all born in '65, '66. I was thirty-five, so maybe I was reborn, but as far as I'm concerned, this life started then. I was a baby and they were babies; we taught each other.

WEIR: Our management, which was a huge and rambling affair involving a lot of people, became aware that the Carousel Ballroom was up for lease. We checked it out, and it looked like the best venue in town. . . . We would do it ourselves, our way, and make sure that nobody misrepresented us or skimmed too much money off the top. We were suspicious of anybody we were dealing with, because we figured they were businessmen, not artists. And why *not* do it by ourselves?

JON McINTIRE [friend and one-time manager of the Dead]: With the Carousel Ballroom, we were trying to do something independently *and* collectively. The Dead started it—Ron Rakow and Rock Scully—but it wasn't the staff of the Dead that ran it then, although all the people were friends. It was the Dead's and the Airplane's home, and a tremendously joyous place to be. We did it because it was a great hall, and it was fun. There was a lot of trust across the board for people—no matter how weird it might look, you would trust that it would come out okay. It was the essence of the Haight-Ashbury scene—before *Time* magazine got hold of it.

HART: The Carousel was our own place, and the familiarity of it was an asset musically. It was *home*. Doing one-nighters, you're exposed to various elements, and there's an uncertainty to your existence. . . .

"Clank your chains and count your change . . ."

McINTIRE: One night we had people burn admission to get in the door—throw money in the fire! They had a choice: burn a dollar or pay five.

At the Carousel we were in a really important developmental stage, musically and technically. At that time, we were children in an adult world, and like children we were doing really desperate things—and it paid great dividends.

HART: It wasn't songs, or entertainment. Most of the time we were playing for salvation . . . playing for *it*. We weren't playing for the $3.50, we were playing because that's what we had to do. We used to call it church, you know.

McINTIRE: The Dead gave me a sense of structure and process that was further advanced than anything I'd ever experienced . . . It brought out emotions I'd never experienced. I became a Deadhead when I heard "The Other One," if I hadn't been one before.

I was into dancing, in between toting ice and counting change at the Carousel. One night this girl and I whirled through each other—realized there is more space than molecules in a body, and utilized that knowledge. It was a far-out night indeed.

47

MARY ANN MAYER

PHIL LESH AND JON McINTIRE IN ENGLAND DURING THE EUROPE '72 TOUR

4
Crazy Fingers

IF YOU GET CONFUSED, LISTEN TO THE MUSIC PLAY

"It's always changing gradually, but sometimes something happens out of the blue. We'll play it one way one night, and the next time we play it, it feels a whole lot different."—BRENT MYDLAND

"Even among musicians, we're an acquired taste. Even if you can perform the kind of music we perform, it's questionable whether you'd want to. We're just those kinds of people."

—Bob Weir

"I will not forgive you
If you will not take the chance . . . "

LESH: Five or six musicians playing together can improvise very complicated music. The structure from which we go the farthest out is a combination of all the different kinds of music we know.

It's like making a stew. You start throwing pieces in, and as it cooks, some pieces take on the characteristics of other pieces. You let it simmer awhile and it blends together, and pretty soon it has a character all its own. Then an idea that's concrete for the six of us will emerge out of all that.

A lick here, a rhythm there, a chord pattern—all the elements of a coherent musical idea will be going on at the same time, but they won't have quite the right time relationship, say. Then all of a sudden it will slide right together, and there it'll be: a complete musical entity; somewhere to start from.

". . . things we've never seen
Will seem familiar"

WEIR: During our plunges through inner and outermost space, we'll get to some rhythmic and tonal mode that suggests a particular song, and one of us will start playing the comp to it. If you can get two on a trip, you generally go there. It can be something we all know, or a completely new idea. We've been playing together so long that it just happens naturally. We're really just playing from the seat of our pants.

KREUTZMANN: We get to live inside each other's minds or playgrounds and we get to do it on a stage for people who are having fun.

49

"Multiplicity is our first characteristic; unity our second."

—Theodore Sturgeon,
More than Human

WEIR: The most I've ever amounted to is through concerted effort with other people. The better I can do for them, the better they'll do for me. That's a pretty consistent lesson life's been hammering me with.

Our understanding of each other and concerted sense of quest coaxes out of us what on a good night I would equate with genius. . . . I've seen what pretty much satisfies my criteria for genius displayed by the various members of the group, almost always in response to a stimulus offered by someone else in the group.

HART: The Grateful Dead listens to the Grateful Dead. . . . We're constantly updating this music as we go along, listening to each other and adjusting from beat to beat, trying to reach this grand agreement as to where it should be. These changes are very subtle, and the audience doesn't hear most of them—until we all adjust into the right place, and then we've *got it*.

GARCIA: It has to do with creating a situation in which miracles can happen, amazing coincidences that all of a sudden put you in a new musical space.

WEIR: Music happens best for us when we rely on our intuitions more and our egos less.

"Some folks trust to reason
Others trust to might
I don't trust to nothin'
But I know it come out right"

LESH: What we do best is improvise, with some kind of spontaneous structure occurring at the time. . . .

MYDLAND: When I first came into the band, Bob said, "One thing you don't want to make the mistake of doing: You don't want to rehearse the material. You know the tune; don't ever play it between gigs. Go do whatever else you want to do . . . rehearsing would just get you stuck in a

groove, and you won't be so open. That's no good."

WEIR: We practice a lot—on stage, in front of people. We practice chasing that elusive goodie.

MYDLAND: Tightness is not what the Dead stands for. If things are too planned out, it can take away my interest. But I like the way we work. It's like going out and doing jam sessions for a living.

KREUTZMANN: Sometimes we describe something without playing it—play *around* an idea instead of playing the exact parts.

HART: We'll play everything *but* the notes . . . we'll play between the notes.

But you're still playing notes.

HART: But we aren't playing the notes that you would suspect we're playing.

◆　　◆　　◆

GARCIA: We've really learned how to play by playing our music together. I wasn't really too much of a guitar player when I started with the

50

band, and what I play now is Grateful Dead guitar. It's grown up with the band.

When I talk about playing, I'm talking about being ready for miracles—being technically able to let it flow. When it's *me* doing it, it's work—but that's a level of competence I like to have. I prefer to play whatever's there at the moment, but I want to be able to rely on my own resources if that's what it comes down to.

THE MYSTERIOUS "ELBOW SEQUENCE," AT BOSTON GARDEN, MAY 1977

WEIR: When I'm on stage playing, I'm not really conscious of the guitar; I'm conscious of the notes and the sounds and the demands of the music. You have to find your voice in the arrangement. You've got to listen to the whole sound and play what the music needs.

MYDLAND: I used to listen to Chick Corea . . . with those full chords and voicings. It used to be that simple chords sounded too easy to me, but now a basic triad really sounds thick. It leaves more room for your imagination, whereas the complex stuff left nothing for the listener to play with.

KREUTZMANN: It's the difference between reading a book and watching the movie. When you read a book, your imagination makes it an incredible experience for you. Our music is like that.

Even if we could lay it down straight we probably wouldn't, because that wouldn't leave any room for intrigues.

> "When I was a young man
> I needed good luck
> But I'm a little bit older now
> And I know my stuff"

GARCIA: People used to notice a tremendous contrast between our good nights and our bad nights. There's still a big difference between our good nights and our not-so-good nights, but even our worst nights are competent now. I walk away from them not feeling nearly as wounded as I used to feel. It isn't nearly as crushing as it used to be.

And more often than not, the whole band feels that *we* [didn't] have a good night, rather than just one of us. That tells me that somewhere along the line our whole esthetic has gotten more focused. I know I've come to appreciate what the other guys are playing and what direction their ideas are taking.

LESH: There is no leader of the Grateful Dead, because it doesn't go Bob's way, it doesn't go my way . . . it goes its own way, as long as it's performing as a unit.

> "Will you come with me?
> Won't you come with me?"

51

WEIR: You have to play with people you like and who will listen to you. And of course, you have to listen to them.

GARCIA: It's not enough just to be good at your instrument—you also have to be able to get along with other musicians. You can't be entirely dogmatic; you can't expect other musicians to play only your music. You have to be flexible. Music stores are full of guys that play really well but can't get along well with other musicians. . . .

◆　◆　◆

Neil Young never played with the Grateful Dead, but his remarks regarding ragged-but-right musicianship are applicable:

"People who feel good to play with are hard to find. I like people who are irregular in their playing, not the guys who play great on a bad day and great plus one on a good day. The guy who plays great on a great day and bad on a bad day—that's the guy I want.

"I'd rather have people who interact with each other and are emotionally connected to what they're doing than a band that's going to play *adequately* every night. I'd rather have a band that I think can explode any time, and I think

---

GARCIA: *You'd be amazed at the mundane levels you never get above, even at the highest concert.*
LESH: *"Oh, shit, my feet hurt!"*
GARCIA: *Right, or "This string doesn't look right."*

---

that's what people like, too. They'd rather hear soul and expression and real fire and emotion than perfection.

"The way I look at it, it's peaks and valleys as opposed to deserts. To go higher, sometimes you have to go lower. Long, flat expanses of professionalism bother me."

MYDLAND: When I was a member of Silver, our manager told us, "You can either rehearse and get really tight and sound like Crosby, Stills and Nash, or you can fuck around and end up sounding like the Grateful Dead."

GARCIA: If there's anything the members of the Grateful Dead share, it's pathological anti-authoritarianism . . . We won't accept leading from each other, much less the world at large.

When you're working in a band, you have to try to let everybody have his own voice the way he sees it. There are always going to be things that create friction.

Part of what's interesting between Weir and me is that he's always going to make musical decisions that I'm not going to agree with fully. But I'll go along with them anyway.

WEIR: Everybody in the Grateful Dead has a fairly individual style. Nobody sounds like anybody else in the group, nor like anybody else. I don't play guitar like anybody I know of; Garcia doesn't play guitar like anybody I know of; Phil doesn't play the bass like a *bass*; the drummers are

BRUCE POLONSKY

BRUCE POLONSKY

plenty quirky; and Brent's unique as well—and getting more bent as the days go by.

Did you think it was going to be like this when you joined the Grateful Dead?

MYDLAND: No. I didn't have any idea.

Could you go back to playing that other way?

MYDLAND: Not the same way, knowing what I do now. It shouldn't be all the same, note for note, every night. If I'm playing for somebody and that's what they're paying me for, fine. But if I was going to put a band together, I'd want everybody to have some input . . .

WEIR: Given any conversation that goes on in this band, there's always going to be another country heard from. Any conversation is going to turn a corner. It's completely unpredictable. I guess we're all gifted with fairly prehensile intellects; I'm not surprised when somebody comes up with some completely off-the-wall lick that just makes sense.

JAY BLAKESBERG

GARCIA: Nobody plays conventionally in the Dead, so everybody has to solve the problem of how to fit into unconventional contexts. Weir and I have a long, serious conversation going on musically, and we've designed our playing to work against and with each other. In a way, his playing puts my playing in the only meaningful context it could enjoy.

"Can't talk to you
Without talking to me . . ."

GARCIA: Weir is an extraordinarily original player in a world full of people who sound like each other. He's got a style that's totally unique, as far as I know. I don't know of anybody else who plays the guitar with the same kind of approach he has to it. That in itself is really a score, I think, considering how derivative almost all electric guitar playing is. I have a hard time recognizing any influence in Weir's playing that I could put my finger on, even though I've been along for almost all of his musical development.

WEIR: My role is a fairly difficult one: being in between the lead and the bass, intuiting where the hell they're going to go, and being there.

When we're playing free, drifting from feeling to feeling and mode to mode, Garcia and Phil are generally playing simple lines. Any combination of two notes suggests a chord. My role and the piano player's role are to be there with that chord, or maybe an augmentation of it. And that might suggest staying there and building on what's happening, or going on to a new key or a new mode. . . .

Sometimes that combination of people guessing leads to some inspirational new idea which is really worth living for.

GARCIA: There are some kinds of passages where Weir's ability to solve the problem of creating a harmonic bridge between all the things going on rhythmically with two drums and Phil's bass style is really extraordinary. He has a really beautiful grasp of altering chords and adding color; he can sneak in other flavors that really influence what I can do.

He's got extraordinarily large hands, so he's able to voice chords that most people can't reach and pull them off so they're just part of the flow of playing. He's playing slide leads quite a bit, and that's neat, too, because it's another context for me to play against.

Did it embarrass you as much as it embarrassed some of the audience that Weir learned to play slide guitar on stage for two or three years?

GARCIA: Yeah, but luckily it didn't embarrass him. . . . Sometimes I like his slide playing. It's so nasty and outrageously raunchy. It's neat, when he hits it.

There's something to be said for the garage-band ethos. Why not learn on stage?

GARCIA: Yeah. It seems like as good a place as any to learn. If I didn't take chances on stage, I don't know where I *would* take them. And the audience certainly gives us that latitude.

WEIR: It's a given that we're going to have to go through some stuff that ain't much fun—such as bad nights—in order to learn how to be more flexible, so that in the end, when we evolve into angels, we can make anything fun. We can make fun out of hell.

54

"When Stephen Stills played with us [Brendan Byrne Arena, East Rutherford, New Jersey, April 1983], he was really moved. He understood the power, and after the gig he said to me—and this is a great compliment, from Stills— 'This is the greatest garage band in the whole world!' He loved the looseness, the spirit. . . . He doesn't get to play with a band that cooks like this. In his band, they're playing his parts. Here, he turns around and these fire-breathing animals are back there doin' the do on his head." —MICKEY HART

LESH: The Grateful Dead used to practice all day. For years and years, we played *every* day—the whole band.

GARCIA [1966]: We try to rehearse every day, because it's the only thing we do, and we want to do it as good as we can. But because we're all human beings and we're all friends, we can't make it be *work*. We can't punch in and play and then punch out.

We try to put in about six hours a day. We get together, and sometimes we might just sit around for an hour or so telling jokes, and then play a little and get some ideas.

HART: In the old days, we'd wake up every day and play. That's what the band was there for. When we had the Potrero Theatre [in San Francisco], we'd go in every day and play.

We'd take a lot of psychedelics and play for long periods of time. We'd get into monstrous jams, truly monumental—they had a life of their own, and never lived again.

GARCIA: When we started working on "The Eleven" in the late sixties, we'd spend hours and hours just playing groups of eleven beats, to get used to that phrase. Then we started working things out in seven, playing patterns and phrases and licks that were two and three seven-beat bars long. We had to do it; you can't play confidently and fluidly in those times without *really* knowing what you're doing . . .

It didn't happen overnight, either. It was a long, slow process that started when Mickey first met Alla Rakha. It was the first time he'd ever heard Eastern players, and he was impressed with their level of technical ability in odd times. . . .

Technique was no problem with Mickey, because he was a champion drummer. His background was . . . more the military trip than band music. For him, the combination of tremendous freedom and tremendous discipline that Indian music has was really impressive, so he started studying with Alla Rakha right away. And that got the rest of us started fooling with ideas. . . .

The challenge was, how do you take these

PETER SIMON

STILLS JOINS THE DEAD ONSTAGE AT THE BRENDAN BYRNE ARENA IN NEW JERSEY, APRIL 1983.

55

meters and translate them to Western body knowledge? Our music is basically in smaller increments—twos and threes and fours. It's harder for Western ears to hear the longer meters.

KREUTZMANN: In "Estimated Prophet" I came up with the idea of putting two seven-beat measures together to make a fourteen-beat phrase. That's a more comfortable length to play with *and* to listen to. It all hangs together because Mickey and I play half-time over it for most of the song, which gives it a natural feel.

"Wo-oh, what I want to know:
Where does the time go?"

WEIR: There are nights when we're playing "Estimated Prophet," or any other tune that's in an odd-time signature, where we get off the *one* [downbeat] and we just can't find it to save our souls. And there are nights when we'll play those same tunes and absolutely no one will play the *one* because everybody always knows where it is.

LESH: I told Brent, "The *one* is always where it *seems* to be."

WEIR: Sometimes the *one* has been lost and given up for dead, everybody's playing their own seven-four and waiting to hear someone resoundingly establish the downbeat, and it actually amounts to something. I guess that's what you'd

BRUCE POLONSKY

"GREAT BANDS HAVE CHEMISTRY . . ."—PHIL LESH

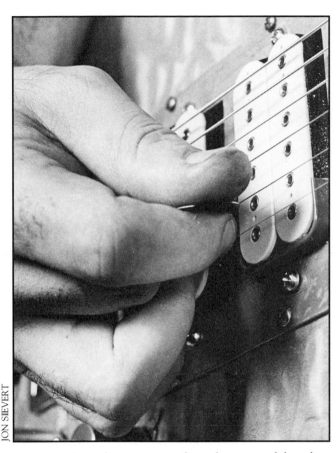

JON SIEVERT

Garcia lost the middle finger of his right hand when he was very young, but the only aspect of his musicianship that's been affected is classical guitar, which requires all five fingers on the picking hand. "The stump is really an extension of my index finger," Garcia explains. "A pick slides right in between so conveniently, leaving both of my picking fingers completely free."

An observer who stationed himself right in front of Garcia at a small club and watched his hands closely says, "I hadn't realized just how much finger-picking he does, but what's most intriguing is the speed with which he changes from flat-picking to finger-picking. Faster than any sleight-of-hand artist, he tucks the pick in between his stump and forefinger—in one smooth, flawless move."

call accidental music, or found art, and by that example there are pleasant surprises to be had on bad nights. . . . We'll go back and listen to the tape and find the basis of another song in there, a genuine phoenix out of the ashes of what was a complete disaster.

GARCIA: We're dealing with several consciousnesses at once—everybody going through their individual changes—and when everybody feels right about it, the form provides openings, then miracles can happen. That's what we're in it for: those moments of *unexpected joy.*

"Did you hear what I just heard?"

LESH: When everybody in the band is happening, there's no time to think about what's going on, no time to think about the notes you're playing. That's when consciousness is a burden.

In my experience, when I suddenly find myself thinking about the notes as I play them, it means I'm not listening.

"I can't stop for nothin'
While I'm playing in the band"

LESH: There's a lot of *playing ahead* in the Grateful Dead, by which I mean that people aren't listening to each other. The drummers get locked into a rhythm, and Jerry will get into a certain scale and play on it until you don't think there's anything else that can be done with it. Sometimes he manages to go farther, but frequently it starts piling up and becomes static. That's the point where if I was playing keyboards or guitar, I could just *turn* things a bit . . .

I will systematically try everything I can think

of—and that's plenty—to make a specific change, and there are times when nothing I do makes any difference. I don't even know whether the other guys in the band are trying as many different kinds of tricks as I am. I'll play more, I'll play less, I'll spread out my registers, I'll try playing one note, and—this gets people really crazy—when I don't have anything to say, or I know that what I do is not going to matter, I will *stop playing.*

But I also know that you can concentrate *too* hard. I should know better, because when it happens best, it's always . . . spontaneous, in a sense.

MYDLAND: Being able to hear everything that's going on on stage has a lot to do with it. There are nights when it doesn't seem to matter what note I play: Just pick one—it's a wrong one. *You lose!* My fingers are going in the wrong spots and I don't know what I can do about it, and I want to get out of the chair for a while because I'm so embarrassed. Then I listen to the tape and find out that it all worked; there was something else I wasn't aware of that made it all fit together.

When everybody's listening to each other and it's blending, it's wonderful. As much as I hate to use the word, it's—*magic.*

GARCIA: I can't say that there's a moment when I'm transformed, when all of a sudden God is speaking through my strings. It's more like, if you practice a lot and play a lot and try to feel right—and if everybody wants it to happen—then there's the possibility that special things will happen. And when they do, everybody gets off on it, not just me. I can get off on a lot of different levels, but *really* getting off is inescapable. Everybody feels it; the audience gets off, the whole band gets off. It becomes one continuous thing.

LESH: And you *can't* put your fingers in the wrong place.

JON SIEVERT

BRUCE POLONSKY

After this many years there's nothing awesome about it at all, except those moments—when you're not a musician anymore, you're not even human. You're just *there*.

KREUTZMANN: I'll come back to the dressing room and look around, look at my hands, and feel I'm high on acid. But I know I'm not; it's the music. Anyway, what's the difference?

I started playing music because it made me feel good, and as soon as I realized that it did that for other people, too, I was hooked.

GARCIA: The ones I love are the ones where it's slippery. The best of everything is all around . . . I don't know how to explain it, but it's *easy*. That's just the coolest feeling in the world.

LESH: When "it" plays instead of me . . . well, as Karl Wallenda put it, "The wire is life. All the rest is just waiting around."

◆　　　◆　　　◆

"The Beast" was first conceived as part of a huge array of percussion instruments assembled

PETER SIMON

ED PERLSTEIN

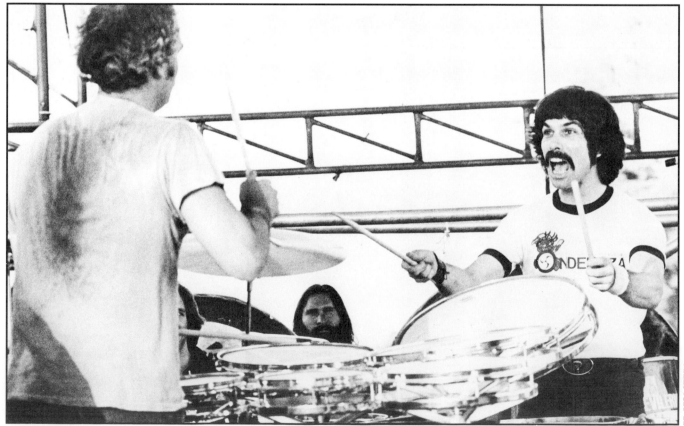

ED PERLSTEIN

63

ED PERLSTEIN

ED PERLSTEIN

WINTERLAND, OCTOBER 1978: HAMZA EL-DIN (*LEFT*), HART, AND SUFI CHOIR MEMBERS. THE AUDIENCE CLAPPED ALONG IN THE TWELVE-BEAT PATTERN.

for the Rhythm Devils' contribution to the soundtrack of the film *Apocalypse Now*. Director Francis Coppola recruited the Dead's drummers to make percussion music in which, according to the liner notes of *The Apocalypse Now Sessions* (Passport Records), "the single breath of war permeated every gesture, every movement, every thing. . . . Music not only relevant to Vietnam in the sixties, but which also extended back in time to the first man" to convey the feeling of the jungle, which Hart characterized as "a constant killing ground" irrespective of human time.

Percussion instruments from all over the world were laid out in the Dead's Club Front studio,

and the musicians—Hart, Kreutzmann, Airto Moreira, Jim Loveless (who built many instruments for the occasion), and others—watched film sequences and crept through the jungle of glass, wood, stone, and metal instruments, choosing and playing spontaneously in response to the visuals and to each other's sounds.

The Beast was part of the Dead's stage setup for several years following the *Apocalypse Now* sessions. It has since been replaced by a smaller version, but many of the percussion instruments are still used during Grateful Dead performances, and the Beast gets a workout at every gig during the drum duet.

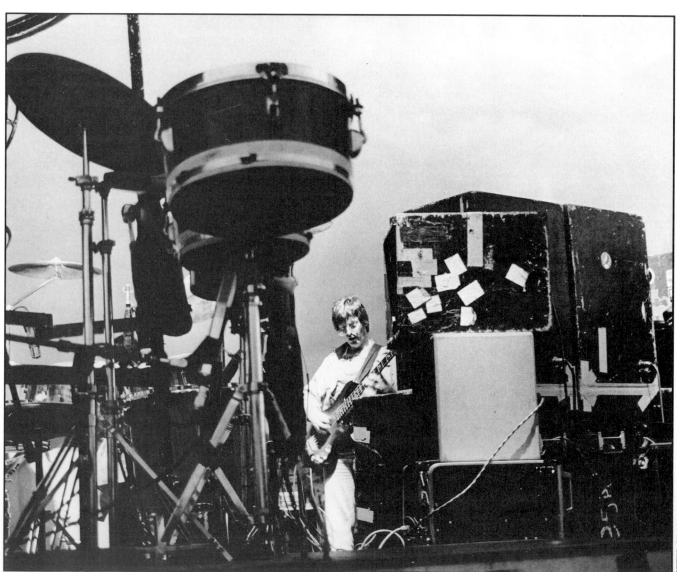

LESH IN JAMAICA, NOVEMBER 1982

PETER SIMON

66

◆   ◆   ◆

KREUTZMANN: Traditionally, drum solos had to be full-bore blowouts——

HART: Ours are conversations, not solos. We're trying to sculpt air.

KREUTZMANN: Both of us are catalysts when we're on stage playing. We just kick each other's tails around.

HART: We take the drum solo as a walk through a particular landscape, what feels like us each time. We're not just there to milk the audience for applause; we don't have to get an overt reaction to know we've moved people. . . .

KREUTZMANN: Our audience listens more.

HART: It's magic when you can bring five thousand people down to just the sound of your fingertip on a drum and then build it back up from a whisper to a scream.

After we got back from Egypt, we played five nights at Winterland [October 17–22, 1978] with the Sufi Choir and Hamza el-Din. The audience actually clapped a twelve-beat pattern. I wouldn't have thought it possible.

KREUTZMANN: It happened again at the Oakland Auditorium [August 5, 1979]. Mickey and Hamza both were playing the tar, and I was playing the talking drum. The audience started clapping in the *weirdest* time! It was just fantastic.

The most fun is being able to communicate in the middle of a concert, changing our ideas right in the moment of the thing, playing with the timing. . . . He'll nod at me, or I'll nod at him.

HART: When we're in the midst of the "battle," just an eye, a look, a flick of the hand will indicate what's needed. There are intuitive responses we have learned over the years that are hard to talk about, but they're there. That's the magic. I wait for those moments.

JERILYN BRANDELIUS

MICKEY HART CHECKS OUT THE BEAST AT FM PRODUCTIONS IN SAN FRANCISCO AS WILLIE JOHN CASHMAN (*FAR LEFT*) AND DANNY ORLANDO, WHO BUILT THE IRON FRAMEWORK, LOOK ON.

◆

5
Dark Star

... FORMLESS REFLECTIONS OF MATTER

"The part of playing when we get off the best is the part that's not repetitive. Some kind of structure is necessary in music if it's going to be communicative at all. It just seems that songs don't go past a certain level." —PHIL LESH

"The challenging part is coming up with structures that have the element of looseness to them, which means they can expand in any direction, go anywhere from anywhere—or come from anywhere—but also have enough form that we can lock into something."

—Jerry Garcia

"Think this through with me
Let me know your mind"

The same experimental spirit that cost the Grateful Dead so much in the studio paid off in their live performances, as evidenced by *Live Dead*, which was recorded at about the time they were in the studio with *Aoxomoxoa*. The first three sides of *Live Dead* represent a nonstop sequence of Grateful Dead music at its highest, going from the unstructured improvisation of "Dark Star" through the well-organized "St.

Stephen" and "The Eleven" and off into the structured but improvisational Pigpen rouser, "Turn on Your Lovelight."

"Dark Star" was recorded in a New York studio in late 1967, during the *Anthem of the Sun* sessions, and released as a single in April of 1968 (backed with a remixed "Born Cross-Eyed"). Lesh recalls that Garcia had little more than some chords and a scrap of paper when he brought it to the band in the studio.

That recording of "Dark Star" consists of two short verses and a repeated chorus, three minutes and five seconds of wispy melody, mumbled lyrics, and suggested tonality, with an organ flourish here and an interesting rhythmic counterpoint between the guitars and the bass there. The studio version wasn't included on any of the studio albums of the period, Lesh recalled in 1984, because "it just moved too fast." He wasn't referring to sales.

The "Dark Star" single was the merest sketch of a framework of a song, but as side one of *Live Dead* proves, that limited form was hardly the

PETER SIMON

70

heart of the matter. What counted was where the Grateful Dead took "Dark Star" in concert once they'd passed through the modest framework.

The *Live Dead* rendition and a few dozen performances captured on tape between 1968 and 1974 stand together as the most compelling evidence of the band's merit as an improvisational ensemble. "Dark Star" never came out the same way twice. Tom Constanten, the avant-gardist composer and keyboard player who played with the Dead in 1969 and 1970, said he "viewed 'Dark Star' as a galaxy that could be entered at any of several places . . . there were a lot of one-of-a-kind moments which were completely spontaneous."

Depending on who was in the band and what was on their minds, "Dark Star" could go just about anywhere. It might turn half a dozen corners, giving glimpses of several scenarios, or it might stick a little closer to home and explore one area more fully. It could be academic or

psychedelic, sentimental and pretty or bombastic and abrasive; and sometimes it hit all those extremes in rapid succession.

"I have a long continuum of 'Dark Stars' which range in character to real different extremes," Garcia told an interviewer in 1972. " 'Dark Star' has meant, while I'm playing it, almost as many things as I can imagine."

" 'Dark Star' is a free entity," Kreutzmann observed. "It has eternity and gives boarding passes, too, but it can be played with a straight feeling, a shuffle feeling, or whatever. It changes.

"It's a total mood indicator: You can tell how everybody is feeling by the way that song is played."

Phil Lesh, brilliant and arrogant, thus never quite a leader of men, was the perfect foil for Garcia's fount of lovely musical ideas. Phil was quick enough to intuit Garcia's moves almost as soon as Garcia himself knew what he was up to, and he was also learned enough to be able to turn his wrong guesses into new twists.

Weir was careful, keeping his musical voice down for the most part but speaking up here and there when he had something to say and could get a chord in edgewise. "When I gained enough momentum, I'd even take the lead," he recalls.

The drummers kept the groove supple and supportive. Fast on its feet and spare with the sticks, the percussion section never retreated into patterns, because that would have forced too much form on the music and it wouldn't have been "Dark Star" anymore. "I played guiro, maracas, gong, drums—all kinds of stuff," says Hart. "We'd go back and forth, each person working on part of the groove, keeping it very light. We tried not to break it up; it was more of a flow from one thing to another."

Pigpen laid out of these jams for the most part. He'd contribute organ textures here and there, but his playing style and his taste in music didn't lend themselves to this brand of exploration. He knew that in due time the music would touch down, and then everybody would be ready for *his* kind of odyssey.

Everything the Grateful Dead members had to say to each other and to the world could be contained in this music, and it never once had to touch the earth with a downbeat or a dominant chord. A good "Dark Star" contains the voices of the players' souls and backbones, chatting and chanting in the polyglot Babel-music that emerged when they brought their many musics together. "Dark Star" sounds like no other music; it sounds like the Grateful Dead.

"It was a time of belonging, of thinking alike, of transcendent sharing. . . . It was a thing together, binding, immortal; it would always be new for them and it would never be repeated."
— Theodore Sturgeon,
More than Human

The Dead couldn't play in the studio the way they played live, even after they'd been doing "Dark Star" for months. It wasn't a matter of drugs or audiences or acoustics or the businesslike ambience of the recording studio; it was all of that and it was none of that. "Dark Star" happened when it happened, and it happened the

PHOTO USED IN AN ADVERTISEMENT FOR SIMBA TALKING DRUMS, JANUARY 1982

way it happened. The group brain went *tabula rasa* at just the right moment (not necessarily the chosen moment, sometimes), and it was "Anybody's choice/I can hear your voice . . . how does the song go?"

♦ ♦ ♦

The range of influences in the band's lexicon can be seen in the tremendous flexibility of "Dark Star," the variety of contexts in which it has been made to fit wonderfully. A few phone calls to

tapers yielded more than twenty-five different songs into which the band has drifted from the far reaches of "Dark Star," among them the classic "St. Stephen," rockers like "Truckin' " and "Casey Jones," percolating, jazzy items like "Eyes of the World" and "China Cat Sunflower," country-flavored songs including "El Paso" and "Me and My Uncle," and the sweetest, quietest of ballads, including "Attics of My Life" and "Stella Blue." The band has also arrived at "Dark Star" from a similarly diverse assortment of musical locales.

The studio version of "Dark Star" and the B-side were included as the "collectible" tracks on an otherwise less-than-illuminating compilation of Warner Bros. Grateful Dead tracks called *What a Long, Strange Trip It's Been*, released in 1977. There are two interesting overdubs at the very end of the song. As a buzz of feedback swells, sibilant speech can be heard; as it fades, a banjo fades in and then out, ending the track.

For the record (or the trivia buffs), the voice is Robert Hunter's and the words are these: "Spin-

ning a set of stars through which the tattered tails of axis rolls about the waxen wind of never set to motion in the unbecoming round about the season hardly matters nor the wise through which the stars were set in spin."

The banjo was neither recorded at the original session nor overdubbed later. "I found an old tape of me playing banjo for a lesson I was giving somebody, in '62 or so," Garcia told Ken Hunt in the British fanzine *Swing '51*. "I threw it on the end of 'Dark Star' just for the hell of it."

◆　　◆　　◆

"It left a smokin' crater
on my mind . . ."

There's another piece with a similarly simple appearance which provides a launching pad for far-reaching group exploration. It's listed in the songbooks as "Cryptical Envelopment" for publishing reasons, but band and fans know it as "The Other One." It's that brief passage of fran-

tic, fearful $12/8$ on side one of *Anthem of the Sun* and side two of the "Skullfuck" album (*Grateful Dead*, the 1971 double live LP) with the perfect paranoia imagery and the perfect scary cartoon soundtrack flavor.

"The thing about 'The Other One' that's so thrilling is that it has all these climaxes at an incredible rate when it's already going at a very strong pace," says Hart.

Never has such black music packed such *joie de vivre!* The visual images are of lovely things turning dangerous ("Spanish lady come to me, she lays on me this rose/It rainbow spiral round and round and trembles and explodes") and of everyday scenes turning fabulously opportune:

"The bus come by and I got on
That's when it all began . . ."

As with "Dark Star," the "song" portion of "The Other One" is straightforward, though characteristically clever, and the sketch of a lyric and the "head" of the song are merely jumping-off points.

"The Other One" has a more clearly circumscribed emotional color than "Dark Star" ("Breathlessness," says Weir, who wrote it). It's a joyful song of terror and a scary song of fun, and in performance the band takes it through many dark passages with brightly lit tonalities close at hand. You can see the cinematic version of "The Other One" in your mind's eye without having to know the words.

HART: "The Other One" was our experiment in polyrhythm. Kreutzmann and I started to do this phasing trip that we called *going out*, where we'd split the band into two sections—three and three or two and four—and then play in revolving patterns of three beats against five, threes against fours, and so on.

We had a tendency to go out before we really knew where we were. . . . When you throw away the basic beats, you have to really know where you are and where everybody else is in relation to each other.

◆　　◆　　◆

This kind of thing wasn't rehearsed or carefully planned out; it was just agreed upon and executed. The players carried ideas forward from their previous encounters with the material and applied whatever was appropriate in the context created by that evening's incarnation of the Grateful Dead.

PIGPEN, 1967

"INTERFERON AND THE DESMODROMES"—PHIL LESH

6
Songwriting

LET MY INSPIRATION FLOW . . .

"The rose is the most prominent image, as far as I'm concerned, as to beauty, delicacy, short-livedness . . . thorniness. . . . There is no better allegory for—dare I say it?—life than roses. Not only do they work, but they never fail. When you put a rose somewhere, it'll do what it's supposed to." — ROBERT HUNTER

"I'd have to admit that most of my favorite Grateful Dead songs are Hunter-Garcia songs. Those guys sound like the Grateful Dead. What the hell?"

—John Barlow

When Arista Records president Clive Davis complained that then-newcomer Brent Mydland's songs for *Go to Heaven* weren't "Grateful Dead enough," Mydland got together with Weir's songwriting partner, John Barlow, and made a few changes. He wasn't sure just how changing "bluebird" to "raven" (in "Easy to Love You") made the song *more* Grateful Dead, but it seemed to appease the record business guy.

Five years later, Mydland says he wouldn't make the change—"I'd come in with a different song instead"—but he admits he now knows what Clive Davis was talking about.

Timeliness of style and accessibility to the hoi polloi are criteria observed by rock bands trying to sell records and get their songs played on the radio. That's the world Mydland came from; the same freedom from commercial concerns that the Dead enjoy as performers allows them to maintain a different set of standards for their songwriting.

Grateful Dead songs don't have to engage the casual ear. Hooks—those devices that make a song catchy and instantly familiar to inattentive listeners—also tend to make a song cloying and boring and irritating in pretty short order. Since the band and the audience already know they're going to be getting together repeatedly, it's more important that the songs be intriguing enough to engage everyone's interest over the long haul, mutable enough to withstand the vagaries of the Grateful Dead's modus operandi, and, well, *vague* enough not to reveal all their verbal and musical charms the first time around. This music makes a certain demand of the listener: that *he* put some thought into it, too.

"Jack Straw" (*Europe '72*), by Bob Weir and Robert Hunter, is a good example of the Dead style. There's a story being played out, but it's never quite clear what the plot is. The characters are a couple of desperadoes, but the dialog never says what made them so desperate.

A very small piece of the action is laid out in the lyric, just enough to pique the listener. "We can share the women, we can share the wine" is a most provocative opening, and "We can share what we got of yours 'cause we done shared all of mine" expresses characterization and plot at once—but the only events depicted take place *between* the incidents that get the two men in trouble.

The picture never stands still nor grows too clear, and from time to time the listener catches a glimpse of it from a new angle that sheds light on the entire song.

These songs ask rather than declare, suggest rather than insist. The musical settings, like the lyrics, are subtle and thought-provoking and never pushy. These songs are clever, sophisticated, decidedly unconventional, and able to stand up to years of perusal, both casual and careful.

An interesting and flexible structure is a *sine qua non* in Grateful Dead songs. The composers leave plenty of room for the players to contribute

musical ideas—or maybe it's that the band *makes* room for themselves.

"When I do a song with the Grateful Dead, I throw it up to them and it's subject to whatever interpretation it gets," Weir said in a 1977 interview. "I don't know anybody who has the energy to tell five other strong-willed musicians, 'Play this, play that.' You get a lot of 'Hey, eat my shorts. I'll play what I feel, man.' So it's pointless to try. And I never get exactly what I imagined."

"We couldn't be more different from each other," Garcia amplifies. "When I put forth an idea, I know that what everyone will play is going to be incredibly different from what I had imagined. . . . There have been times when that has really made me flip out. If I thought a piece of material was delicate, and suddenly there was some weird idea stuck into it . . . holy shit!"

When Brent Mydland taught "Easy to Love You" (also on *Go to Heaven*) to the Dead, "I told Jerry what I wanted him to play on the intro," he recalls with a slight laugh. "He added a couple of grace notes and made it his, but he used the melody I wanted. But I couldn't imagine doing that now."

◆   ◆   ◆

Whether it's embraced heartily, accepted with resignation, or resisted tooth and nail, the creating in the Grateful Dead is done collectively all the way. The music follows its own nose and goes *its* way, pursuing the novel and shunning the familiar. "A lot of the material could be hits, whatever that means," comments Mydland, "but then the Grateful Dead gets hold of it and says, 'Uh-oh, that sounds too normal. Let's fuck with it.'"

Mydland wasn't too comfortable with that aspect of Grateful Dead music at first. "There are places in 'Sugar Magnolia' where a certain chord would fit in naturally, but Bob put in different ones. I asked him once why he'd put some weird chord where another one would go right in, and he said, 'That's my signature lick. That makes it my sound. *Anybody* could have stuck those other chords in there.'"

ALLEN MESSICK

JOHN BARLOW AT HOME IN WYOMING

The Dead didn't write a lot of songs at first. Pigpen, Garcia, and Weir came from the country, folk, and blues traditions, which have rich catalogs of standards from which to draw material. When the jug band went electric, much of their repertoire was adapted from the same sources as before; with the acid experiments came the urge to experiment with words and music of their own.

"Our ideas about writing songs are not particularly affected by rock and roll," Garcia noted in a 1966 interview. "None of us was really playing that much rock and roll before we got together as a band. We have material that comes from all different areas, and somehow we can make the stuff work. We're going in as many directions as we can go."

Robert Hunter and John Barlow, respectively

"Weir has his own particular style of phrasing things, which I've always thought sounded a bit like the way a man would walk if he had two pairs of knees. But it seems to work." —JOHN BARLOW

Garcia's and Weir's collaborators, were poets and novelists who happened to be long-time friends of the musicians; they were drafted (Barlow a few years after Hunter) into the songwriting ranks. Neither was drawn to the Tin Pan Alley model of songwriting, in which a song is merchandise first and art if possible.

79

ED PERLSTEIN

HUNTER POSES IN FRONT OF A GIANT *BLUES FOR ALLAH* COVER AT THE DEAD'S STUDIO, CLUB FRONT, IN SAN RAFAEL, CALIFORNIA.

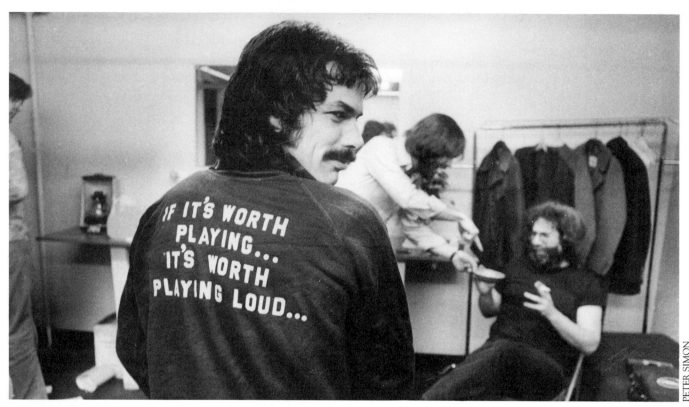

PETER SIMON

80

MARY ANN MAYER

ROBERT HUNTER, 1972

Hunter was away from the Bay Area when he received Garcia's request for lyrics. He sent "Alligator" and "China Cat Sunflower" from New Mexico, and when he returned to California, he joined the band as a non-performing member, collaborating with Garcia and occasionally Lesh.

> "Crazy cat peeking through a
>   lace bandanna
> Like a one-eyed Cheshire
> Like a diamond-eyed jack . . ."

HUNTER: I think the germ of "China Cat Sunflower" came in Mexico, on Lake Chapala. I don't think any of the words came, just the rhythms. I was writing things to these rhythms, and subsequently I put some of the rhythms to these images.

At one point I had a cat sitting on my belly, and I was in a rather hypersensitive state. I followed the cat out to—I believe it was Neptune, but I'm not sure—and there were rainbows across Neptune and cats marching across this rainbow.

All right, I wrote part of it in Mexico and part of it on Neptune!

Did the Grateful Dead's version come out rhythmically the way you felt it when you wrote it?

HUNTER: Not at all.

Hunter ran downstairs and fetched his acoustic guitar. He played a very folky sounding chord pattern with a nursery-rhyme strum, and in a voice likewise gentle sang two verses that aren't part of the song as recorded and performed by the Dead, followed by the three familiar verses, and then two more. These last eight lines became the counting-down descant in "The Eleven," the first Lesh–Hunter collaboration. "The Eleven" appears on *Live Dead*, which was recorded at the Avalon Ballroom at the same time the band was in the studio making *Aoxomoxoa*, which includes "China Cat." However modest Hunter's musical setting for the piece, it yielded substantial material for the Grateful Dead—although Garcia claims those early songs were unsuccessful:

GARCIA: A lot of the *Aoxomoxoa* songs are overwritten and cumbersome to perform. They're packed with lyrics or musical changes that aren't worth it for what finally happens with the song. But at that time, I wasn't writing songs for the band to play—I was writing songs to be writing songs.

Those were the first songs Hunter and I did together, and we didn't have the craft of songwriting down. We did things that in retrospect turned out to be unwise, from the point of view that it's important that the musicians enjoy playing the tune. When you write a song that's a chore to play, the performances never sound anything but strained.

There's technically too much happening in a song like "Cosmic Charlie" for us to be able to come up with a version of it that's comfortable to sing *and* play on stage. I never would have thought about that when I started writing songs; I didn't realize you had to think about that stuff.

"Cosmic Charlie" is a recording song. Its weaknesses are part of what's musically clever about it, but also part of what's cumbersome about performing it. The last time we worked it out was in 1976 [with Donna Godchaux singing], and it was effective—sort of. We had a hell of a time getting through it, and the fact that it didn't stick as a piece of material tells me it's flawed. It's not quite *performable*. Most of the *Aoxomoxoa* songs have

81

PETER SIMON

worked their way out of our repertoire; nobody in the band really expresses any interest in playing them. . . . Even "China Cat Sunflower" is marginal.

When Bob Weir got the urge to begin writing in earnest, he and Hunter undertook to work together. They produced a handful of excellent songs, including "Playing in the Band," "Sugar Magnolia," "Jack Straw," and "Greatest Story Ever Told."

♦ ♦ ♦

WEIR: "Greatest Story Ever Told" started out with a pump at Mickey's house. He was working on a solo album [*Rolling Thunder*, 1972], and he gave me a tape of the pump and told me to write a song to the rhythm.

I built a chord structure around the pump tape. Mickey had suggested that the lyric be patterned after "Froggy Went A-Courtin' and He Did Ride," and Hunter came up with "Moses come ridin' up on a guitar." I patterned the melody after "Froggy Went A-Courtin'," too. And that's the "Pump Song" [on *Rolling Thunder*, 1972, featuring the Tower of Power horns, Garcia on "insect fear" guitar, and others].

WEIR AND BARLOW MAKE LIKE COWBOYS, MILL VALLEY, CALIFORNIA, 1972.

Why did you change guitar to quasar for the version of the song on your first solo album [Ace, 1972]?

WEIR: Because I liked *quasar* better.

HUNTER: Weir didn't want to sing "Moses come ridin' up on a guitar," so I changed it to "quasar." He said that was great, but I subsequently thought, "Wait—*quasar* doesn't fit the song in any way. *Guitar* is a wooden image; it fits the textures."

And "Greatest Story Ever Told" wasn't my title for the song, either. Weir came up with that.

WEIR: I called the song "Greatest Story Ever Wrote." I don't know how it got changed to "Greatest Story Ever Told." Must have been a clerical error on the album copy.

HUNTER: If I were going to write a song called "The Greatest Story Ever Told," it would be that song. That song was "Moses."

Is this the kind of thing you were thinking of when you said, "Weir uses a lyricist like a whore"?

HUNTER: Well, he makes you work an awful lot. When I'm working, I like to follow my own directions. The criticism I'll take is pretty much limited to, "Could you improve the way you said this? It doesn't sing too well." I'll go back to find a different way to say what I said.

If they say, "Would you not say that?" or "Would you say something different?" often I don't like to do that, but I will. . . .

I have a tendency not to want to write the sort of things Weir wanted in his songs at that time. He wasn't looking for the telling phrase, the really apt combination of words to fire off a thought or an emotional process; he was more interested in water color, the textures of the words.

WEIR: That may have been true when Hunter and I were working together, in the early seventies, but my appreciation of poetry is a whole lot more developed now.

"You know better but I know him"

Their differences in taste and methods made writing together difficult and ultimately unsatisfying to both Weir and Hunter, so Weir recruited his old prep-school chum, John Barlow.

BARLOW: Bobby said, "Well, you write poetry—you might try your hand at writing lyrics." I wasn't doing anything else, so I did try my hand. I'm not sure Hunter was too enthusiastic about there being another Grateful Dead lyricist, but on the other hand, he did tell me rather pointedly to take Weir *with his blessing.*

So I sort of made up some things that sounded like lyrics. The first one was "Mexicali Blues," and I was just *stricken* when I heard what kind of setting he'd chosen for it. It turned out to be okay after I got over the initial shock.

> "Cherish well your thoughts
> And keep a tight grip on your
> booze . . ."

BARLOW: It is not easy to write with somebody, but it does have a certain advantage in spite of the turmoil that goes on. There's something two people can often do that one person can't. Two entirely different points of view come together in a way that may not be all that pleasing to either one of the authors but works in a way that their individual visions may not.

It's a lot like being married: Sometimes we can't stand each other over what are fundamentally esthetic differences. But fortunately, we've been friends for so long that, as with being married, we've got fallback positions if things get too scary.

The way I like to work—and what usually happens—is one or the other of us has an idea which is not well-developed, and we develop it more or less simultaneously. That gives us each the opportunity to make even-handed contributions to what the other is doing rather than make unilateral changes later.

Often the first thing I hear of a song is the rhythm part. He usually says he'll work out the melody. That's made for occasions when I've been able to contribute melodic ideas, but it is a little more demanding that way.

GARCIA: A lot of times with Weir, the melody is the last thing to get composed. That's backwards from the way I do it, and you can tell, because a lot of times Weir's songs are arrangement-strong and melody-weak.

Every once in a while he gets a real good one where the whole thing is really graceful. "Estimated Prophet" is a well-conceived, well-written song. But for the most part, the sung melody is where people have the hardest time getting access to Weir's songs. . . . They don't always have the kind of happy marriage of lyric and melody you find running through your head.

BARLOW: On occasion I've given him a set of lyrics and he's taken them someplace. It hasn't always been someplace I wanted to see them go, but they've gone there anyway. And there have been a number of really serendipitous cases where I've given Weir a set of lyrics just knowing I was going to see my baby slaughtered before it was over, and it's come out just right.

HUNTER: It's become so much more delightful to be alive and involved with the creative process since I stopped worrying about what happens to this stuff after it leaves my typewriter. I put the best I can into that work, and I'm damned if I'm gonna sit around and cry about it or hassle about it later.

Before you get into being a precious artist about these things, you have got to be a craftsman.

Say you're a carpenter and somebody wants

83

ROGER RESSMEYER

some shelves, and you come in with this *beautiful* door. There it is in a nutshell. Craftsmanship is the first thing in being a songwriter; if you're a good enough craftsman, eventually that aspect of it will become taken for granted and you can be more and more the artist.

"Now and again these things just got to be done"

BARLOW: There's a song on *Ace* called "Walk in the Sunshine," which neither Weir nor I is terribly fond of. He didn't like the lyric, and time was running out on the album. My father had just died and I had to go home, so Weir's old lady set me up with a bottle of whiskey and some other catalysts for one last twenty-four-hour plunge at trying to come up with something new. But nothing would come.

I had just read *The Dwarf* [the 1945 novel by the Swedish author Pär Lagerkvist]. I managed to write a lyric to the "Walk in the Sunshine" music based on the nasty little man in that story.

"Hustle for me, Ace
Finish in first place
I got a plan that'll set us up fine
A piece of the action
Is all that I'm askin'
I'll see you get yours
When I see I've got mine"

BARLOW: All I wanted was for it to be so ugly that "Walk in the Sunshine" would look good by comparison. It worked.

"Would you hold it near,
As it were, your own?"

BARLOW: I had the notion of "Money Money" as a Mose Allisoney kind of jive blues. . . . It came out sounding like Mose Allison done by Grand Funk Railroad. I was really upset by that for a while and refused to write any lyrics without hearing the music first. I got stubborn and decided that my judgment regarding what music meant was better than Weir's judgment regarding

BANNER DISPLAYED BY DEADHEADS AT THE OAKLAND AUDITORIUM IN OAKLAND, CALIFORNIA, IN DECEMBER 1982

DAVID GANS

what words meant. That was kind of a silly attitude.

> "Knockin' off my neighborhood
> savings and loan
> To keep my sweet chiquita in
> eau de Cologne
> She wants money . . ."

Why did the Dead only perform "Money Money" live those few times in the Northwest in '74?

WEIR: Well, a couple of people in the band didn't like the little story in that song, which—though tongue-in-cheek—they didn't think was as funny as I thought it was. So we just put that one away.

"I just don't see why the bounds of popular music should be so constricting as to deny the possibility of, for instance, odd time signatures or harmonic modes." —BOB WEIR

> "You and me bound to spend
> some time
> Wond'rin' what to choose"

GARCIA: I'm a better editor than writer. I do some writing, but I've never developed the necessary discipline to write graceful lyrics. I usually find that if I have an idea that needs to be expressed in words, Hunter can express it better than I can.

He and I don't clash. . . . We both tend to focus on the work. *Choosing* a lyric to sing is really about as much responsibility as I would want to have toward the content of a song.

HUNTER: Garcia's muse will visit me and say, "Here's a song for Garcia. If he doesn't appreciate it or do something with it, *then* you can have it. But you've got to give him first choice on it."

I write differently for Garcia than I do for myself. I see what he does and doesn't do out of

what I've given him over the years, and I've gotten a bit of a suss of what he feels he can speak comfortably.

I know through long experience the sorts of things he *doesn't* like to sing about—that don't express *him*. There's a kind of revolutionary rhetoric that he just finds distasteful. I've tried it on him, but he's just put those things away and forgotten about them.

There's a range of emotions he doesn't like to talk about, and certain ways of relating that aren't his ways. I wouldn't write for Garcia, "I'm comin' to getcha, honey, I'm gonna getcha, yeah, yeah, yeah!" You can't imagine Garcia singing that, can you?

> "If you can abide it
> Let the hurdy gurdy play"

HUNTER: We have worked a hundred different ways, but Garcia generally prefers to be given just the lyrics even though I generally write them as *songs*. He'll express his objections to the lyric—what he doesn't like in it or wants more or less of, what he wants changed—and I'll either argue or rewrite to specifications.

GARCIA: Some songs are real slow-growing, and some are moments of inspiration. I can't make them happen.

Every once in a while one pops out. BAM! All of a sudden it's there. "Wharf Rat" was almost instantaneous, and so was a big part of "Terrapin." Both of those fell on incredible coincidences: Just about the time I had those musical ideas worked out to show to Hunter, he happened to have lyrics that fit perfectly, with a little fooling around.

HUNTER: With something like "Touch of Grey," which is a bit difficult, he may say, "How do you do this?" to get an idea of how it rolls along as a song. I'll reach for his guitar to show him some chords, and he'll say, "Wait, wait, wait. On second thought, don't play it for me, because when you do, it takes a couple of weeks for your changes to get out of my mind so I can get to business with it." He wants to create his own thing around the lyric.

85

GARCIA: Hunter sang "Touch of Grey" as a sort of dry, satirical piece with an intimate feel, but I heard something else coming through it. "We will get by" said something to me, so I set it to play big. My version still has the ironic bite in the lyrics, but what comes across is a more celebratory quality.

LESH: It was the same hassle with my songs: There was too much going on in them. My songs are too complicated to get what the Grateful Dead's good for out of them.

Garcia will bring his groove in and we'll be comping along before he even sings a word or plays the chord changes through.

But Bob has to explain his songs to the band, so why is it a problem for you to come in with a realized composition?

LESH: It bores me.

What I don't want is their undivided attention. I don't want them sitting there saying, "Yes, Phil. What's the next note?"

♦　　♦　　♦

LESH: I gave up songwriting after *Mars Hotel,* because the results were so disappointing. "Unbroken Chain" could have been really something. Some people think it really is, but I wanted it to be what I wanted it to be. . . . It just didn't happen, so I decided to concentrate on playing the bass as best I can.

The only reason I made up "Passenger" [*Terra-*

EILEEN LAW AT HER DESK IN THE DEAD OFFICE IN SAN RAFAEL, CALIFORNIA

pin Station] was that I wanted the guitar players to play with a little raunch. . . .

I can't get what I want from the band, and I don't want to lean on them, because I know it would be counterproductive. You have to depend on the people in the band to play the song, and you can't afford the luxury of arrogance. It won't work—*especially* in the Grateful Dead. Most people will say everybody contributes something, but it's never quite what you imagined when you wrote the song.

This attitude might seem strange in such an articulate proponent of collective creation, but Lesh was a "serious" composer, albeit in rather esoteric realms, before he joined the Grateful Dead. His *komponist* mentality caused him some frustration in college, when some of his pieces proved difficult to perform to his satisfaction. Lesh confesses that one of the most attractive features of the electronic music he discovered while at the College of San Mateo at the start of the sixties was that it freed him from the need for performers.

Asked in November of 1984 whether he'd ever be able to reconcile his composer's dogmatism with the Grateful Dead's chaotic method of absorbing material, he responded, "Maybe I'm learning. I've discovered that Brent and I can sing together and have a blend."

Their collaboration began with a couple of raunchy performances of the Beatles' "Why Don't We Do It in the Road" on the summer and fall '84 tours. They hadn't completed an original song by the Halloween week gigs at Berkeley, but the pair did rehearse and perform the old Spencer Davis tune "Gimme Some Lovin' " as a vocal duet, to the instant and resounding delight of the fans. "I heard that famous roar comin' back at us when we started that," Lesh said shortly after the show. "I've heard it for the Grateful Dead, and I've heard it for other groups, but that was the first time I ever heard it while I was singin' lead!"

♦　　♦　　♦

"Sometimes the songs that we hear
Are just songs of our own"

BLAIR JACKSON

HUNTER: I'd really prefer not to get into tearing apart the symbology of my own songs, and I'll tell you why: If there were a better way to say things than with symbols, you'd say them that way.

A symbol, by its very nature, can pull in many shades of meaning, depending on the emotional tone with which you engage the piece.

I assume that over the years you've heard exotic interpretations of your lyrics that had absolutely nothing to do with anything you've thought about them.

HUNTER: That is one reason I'd rather not print the lyrics. You know, people hear their own songs. If you can cue them into their own thought processes, then later—when they find out what the words really are—they might realize that it was their own interpretation they were listening to. I *like* that. That's why I don't print the lyrics.

GARCIA: Sometimes I don't notice the sense of a lyric for *years*. Then I feel like the biggest dummy 'cause I didn't even know a song was about that thing.

"Let the words be yours
I'm done with mine"

BARLOW: It took me a long time to get to the point where I could hear somebody say they really liked a song which I felt had come off poorly and not say to them, "I thought it was a piece of shit." What I say now is, "Thank you. I appreciate that. What do you suppose it means?" And the interesting thing is that usually what they come up with is entirely different from what I had in mind.

In some cases the interpretation reported by someone sounds even better than what I really had in mind, so I tell them, "Yeah, that's what it means." What they've essentially done is write their own song.

I *hate* to say what "Cassidy" is about, because Deadheads have given me ideas that are superior in many ways to what I had in mind when I started writing the words.

"What you are, what you're
meant to be"

EILEEN LAW [the band's Deadhead liaison and a close friend since the Warlocks days]: I lived in a tent behind Weir's house when I was pregnant, and I'd hear him playing these beautiful riffs in the house while I practiced my breathing exercises.

WEIR: While she was having the child, I was sitting out in the living room, scratching on the ol' guitar, and this song just kinda made its presence known. I named it "Cassidy" because it was born the same day as Cassidy Law.

LAW: I had decided on the name before she was even born, because I thought it sounded good for either a boy or a girl. I don't think she's ever really liked the name, though.

WEIR: I had the song for about a year and a half before I started on my solo album.

LAW: Hunter was going to write some lyrics about a card game, and I said, "No, no, that's not what that tune is about." Barlow came out here from Wyoming on his motorcycle around that time, and the next thing I knew he and Bobby had this song.

BARLOW: I was thinking about Neal Cassady's departure and Cassidy Law's arrival as being part and parcel of one another—not like reincarnation, but more the way the cycle works. So what that song is, is a wave goodbye to Neal and a hallo to Cassidy.

WEIR: Barlow finished it about a week before we recorded it. I folded up the paper and put it in my pocket.

I recorded a basic track with my guitar and Billy's drums, and then I overdubbed a couple of rhythm guitars and a lead track. It added up to this sort of lush, slightly out-of-tune, angular sound I wanted. When I broke out the words and applied them to the melody—for the first time, really—they fit perfectly. By the second verse, Donna was singing harmony. The whole thing was relatively effortless.

7
Recording, Part 1

ALL GRACEFUL INSTRUMENTS ARE KNOWN

"They concentrate on live shows rather than the recording process . . . they prefer the moment to the artifact." —THE ROLLING STONE ENCYCLOPEDIA OF ROCK & ROLL

"What we do is play for people, for warm human bodies. We don't play so good for machines." —Jerry Garcia

Since their 1967 debut, *The Grateful Dead,* the band and individual members have released more than fifty discs, the only common denominator among them being their experimental nature. Something new is going on at one level or another—or several—in everything the Dead do. As with songwriting and performing—and everything else they do, really—recording is something to experiment with and experience on its own terms, not merely a means to an end.

They've recorded in dozens of studios, including a couple of their own; they've tried unconventional and experimental techniques with both live and studio recordings and on several occasions combined material from both kinds of sources; they've cut 'em fast and they've cut 'em slow. And everybody in the band agrees that

THE PRODUCER WAS UNPREPARED FOR THE SOUND OF TC'S PREPARED PIANO

although many of the Dead's records have been satisfying—if not to listen to when completed, then at least as recording experiences—only in a few instances have the Grateful Dead managed to capture on vinyl what they create in concert.

◆ ◆ ◆

GARCIA: The record is one of the forms that music can take, but it's not a reflection of what *we* do. If you're an artist, lithographs might be what gets you off the most, but if you have to do a gouache you do a gouache. So we just treat recording as what it is.

I prefer playing live. It's definitely a richer experience: You play a note and you can see where it goes, what the response is. That's true in the studio, too, but you're doing it with other musicians. What we might be interested in as musicians might not relate to anybody else. Having a group of musicians in a studio is not unlike having a room full of plumbers.

LESH: Our performances on record are always merely adequate. We don't really *dive into it* in a recording studio. You know what happens when you start to dive into something? It comes out so much like music that it can't be a record. You get ahead of the click [metronome] track, and you may go back to it or even get behind it a little bit. You can't have that if you're going to overdub things later—according to conventional "wisdom," that is.

GARCIA: I try to psych myself up in the studio—getting a nice, tasty stereo mix in the headphones and closing my eyes and kind of imagining, projecting myself into an audience situation, but it doesn't work. It *has* to be a two-way street: The audience is hoping to get off, and we're hoping to click.

We used to talk to Bill Walton, the basketball star, about being *on*—hitting it just right. There's a great correlation between music and professional sports. They're both improvisational.

WEIR: It might be a viable direction for us to come up with a bunch of material, go in, and just jam like we do on stage and put out records like jazz people do—and not expect to sell very many of them but end up with a pretty fair catalog.

KREUTZMANN: Industry people laugh at us and say, "Those guys are nuts—they're not out there trying to get top singles." It's easy to say we don't care. We *do* care, a lot—but not about what's supposedly important, like how many records we sell. None of that ever worked for us . . . but the Deadheads sure have!

"Mama, mama, many worlds
I've come
Since I first left home . . ."

GARCIA: Our first album was done in like three nights and mixed in one day in LA. We really didn't much care about it while we were doing it.

At that time, we had no real *record* consciousness. We were just going to go down to LA and make a record. We had a producer—Dave Hassinger—we had chosen because he'd been the engineer on a couple of Rolling Stones records that we liked the sound of. . . .

We played some pretty hyperactive music——
LESH: That Ritalin-and-hashish sound. . . .
GARCIA: That record has its sort of crude en-

ergy, but the temp was way too fast. I can't enjoy it, really. The songs were simply what we were doing on stage—but on stage the tunes lasted longer because we like to play a lot. When you're dancing and getting high, you can easily dance to a half-hour tune and even wonder why it ended so soon.

The second record went the whole other way. We were going to work on it, make sure it sounded good, really get into recording and go on some trips with it. We recorded for a couple of weeks in LA, experimentally, and accomplished absolutely nothing.

Then we went to New York . . . and got our producer [Hassinger again] so excited that he quit. We were being so weird, and he was only human, after all, and didn't really have to go through all that. . . .

WEIR: The first album was recorded on a three-track. With eight tracks for the second one, the possibilities seemed limitless. So we started getting kinda nuts.

Tom "TC" Constanten, Lesh's buddy from Cal and Mills College, was brought in to add a little "prepared piano" to the suite that was to constitute side one of the album.

TC: The final part of "That's It for the Other One" was an overlay of several live performances, whence it gets that incredible depth; it's a remarkable effect. They wanted to take that up and swirl it into an explosion, and out of the ashes of that would stealthily enter the warm, misty waves of "New Potato Caboose."

At one point I dived into the piano, having pulled the string on a gyroscope and put it against the sounding board. The sound is not unlike that of a chainsaw being taken to it. I wasn't able to see it because of the sightlines in the studio, but I'm told that Hassinger cleared his seat by fully a foot and a half when he heard it. They managed to calm him down, however, and actually the piano wasn't damaged at all.

LESH: We didn't really want to scare him half to death—we just forgot to tell him. That kind of stuff was normal, to us.

". . . I came across an empty space"

WEIR: We were recording in New York. Things were going kinda slow, because we were getting crazy. Dan Healy was engineering, at our insistence and Hassinger's reluctance, and the two of them weren't getting along particularly well.

There was a great deal of confusion and hassling over just doing the songs ("No, I want it weirder!" "The boys in the band want to get *out there*!"), and Dave Hassinger wanted to get the record done within the budget, et cetera, like any good producer should.

I had a song called "Born Cross-Eyed." We'd more or less done the basic track and some overlays, and I was describing how I wanted the song. There was a little bit of tension in the studio, but I was oblivious to it; I was into brown rice at the time and wasn't taking any drugs—zero—but I was pretty spaced, anyway.

I was describing how I envisioned the song, and Healy and Hassinger were hassling over something. The song got quiet at one point, and so I announced, "Right here I want the sound of thick air." I couldn't describe it back then, because I didn't know what I was talking about. I do know now: a little bit of white noise and a little bit of compression. I was thinking about something kind of like the buzzing that you hear in your ears on a hot, sticky summer day.

So I said, "Dave, right here I want the sound of thick air."

Dave Hassinger threw up his hands and said, "Thick air. He wants the sound of THICK AIR. *Thick air!* He wants the sound of thick air"—over and over again, as he's walking out of the studio.

That was the end of Dave Hassinger and the Grateful Dead. It wasn't exactly my fault, but I think I was the straw that broke the camel's back.

"One man gathers what another man spills"

GARCIA: So Phil and I, mostly, worked and worked for about six months. We assembled live tapes and went through the most complex operations you can go through in a recording studio. . . . And Dan Healy, who is real fast on his feet, was able to come up with some crazy things.

LESH: We worked for about six months at Columbus Recorders, smoking a lot of pot and putting all these two-track tapes of gigs together. We used stuff from the Great Northwest tour with Quicksilver, where we played our asses off with this material—*really* hot. We lost generation upon generation upon generation from overdub-

---

You don't mind people taping your music in concert?
GARCIA: *Not particularly.*
That seems to be defeating the idea of selling records.
WEIR: *Well, if we ever make a really good record, then probably they'll rush out and buy that anyway.*
GARCIA: *The shows are never the same, ever. And when we're done with it, they can have it.*

---

bing; that's why it's so funky sounding. But that adds to that sort of pillow of sound.

The gig that became the core tape of *Anthem of the Sun* was the one Garcia talked about in the movie, where he "threw me down the stairs" because I stopped playing for a while. I got lost and stopped. I couldn't figure out what was going on.

There were three steps up to a narrow door. After the set I just wanted to get past Garcia and get out of there, put my bass in the case and go home.

He said, "Motherfucker, you *play*"—mumble mumble. He just kinda pushed me out of the way.

That was the first act of violence that any one of us had ever directed toward another one. It blew my mind, for about six or eight hours. . . . "You ever touch me again . . ." You know how it is.

And of course, the first thing he said to me the

next day was, "Hey, I'm sorry," and I said, "Hey, forget it." That's all you can really say.

That was one night we weren't high on acid. We were just *playin'*. If you're not on drugs and you play shit like that, I dunno—maybe it makes you wired-er, more edgy. We were trying too hard. . . .

The tape was so hot that we didn't connect it with that incident for a while. I think Jerry was the first one who recognized it. He told me about it, and I said, "Are you shittin' me?"

Even after all that misunderstanding, we used *those* tapes of that night: St. Valentine's Day, 1968, at the Carousel Ballroom. We used that for the core of "The Other One," and "Alligator," too.

TAPING A TV SHOW IN SAN FRANCISCO, CIRCA 1967. PHIL PLAYS A BROOMSTICK INSTEAD OF HIS BASS IN PROTEST OF THE LIP-SYNCHING ARRANGEMENT.

JIM MARSHALL

WEIR: The names of the songs on the first part of side one ["That's It for the Other One" and its four oddly named segments] were all just made up for publishing purposes. TC made up most of those names . . . at points where we could say it had clearly changed. Otherwise we would only have gotten publishing money for one song.

The songbook says, "While skippin' through the lily fields/I came upon an empty space," but I only sang it that way once or twice. Ever since then it's been "*escaping* through the lily field."

HART: We started "Born Cross-Eyed" on the second beat and left the *one* completely blank. That made everything in the song seem off-kilter. It's a rhythmic and aural illusion; it tricks the ear.

LESH: "Born Cross-Eyed" also has the only recorded example of my trumpet playing, a little Miles Davis "Sketches of Spain" bit I overdubbed in the break where Weir sings, ". . . from time to ti-ime . . ."

Anthem of the Sun is my favorite Grateful Dead album, because that really describes it, for me. That one and *Live Dead.*

I have to admit that remixing *Anthem* was a mistake. The next time it comes out, we'll go back to the original mix. Oh man! That mix is a work of art.

"We can have high times if you'll abide"

Work on the Dead's third album was well under way with eight-track tape recorders when the first sixteen-track machines became available. They used one at the Avalon Ballroom without a mixing console, correctly assuming that the shortest path from microphone to tape would yield the cleanest recording. The result, *Live Dead,* was the first live record ever made with sixteen-track equipment.

On the other hand, the band thought nothing of scrapping the eight-track work they'd done in the studio and starting over with the new gear. One of their experiments was "Barbed Wire Whipping Party," which included a sixteen-track cascade—sound recorded on one track was played back a split second later and rerecorded on the next track, then played back another split second later, and so on. "We all had microphones and headphones and hoses coming from a tank of nitrous oxide," Garcia recalls, laughing. "When you'd say something, it came back sixteen times. You can imagine how confusing that was on nitrous oxide—immediately it turned into total gibberish."

"Barbed Wire Whipping Party" was not included on the album *Aoxomoxoa,* but plenty of weird stuff was. Another piece that was heavily influenced by nitrous oxide is "What's Become of the Baby," a deeply psychedelic lyric that Lesh calls "a raunch classic."

"I had a concept in my head, but I had no idea of how to do it technically or how to communicate it," Garcia recalls. "I wanted to contain the whole band just playing music inside the voice, where you'd hear some kind of Grateful Dead randomness replacing the voice, a guy opening his mouth and the Grateful Dead coming out. I know how to do it now, but it was impossible then."

93

CHAPTER

8
Gigs

THERE'S A BAND OUT ON THE HIGHWAY

"It's like comparing being in a rowboat on the ocean with building a ship in a bottle. Making a record is very picky, compulsive stuff. Playing music for live human beings is something real. It's much more fun." —JERRY GARCIA

"Generally, the bigger the crowd the sloppier we play."

—Bob Weir

"Wherever he goes the people all complain"

GARCIA: By the late sixties we were on the road a lot, so we were no longer part of a stable local community. We were now nomads, traveling around America, and at that time lots of parts of America had never experienced anything strange at all. We were the first weird people a lot of those places ever saw.

We sort of fell away from the world at large and concentrated on our own survival. It seemed like the smart thing to do. The big world is too hard-edged. It has too many things that don't work out quite right for us. But at least it lets us happen.

"Dressed myself in green . . ."

WEIR: A friend's father had a cabin on the Russian River. We packed up and went to that place and worked up a few songs, among them the first few strains of "The Other One," "Alligator," and a few others.

We had a little platform that I guess was for a tent, on a bluff over the river. We used that for a stage—set up all our equipment and the PA so it was facing the river. You couldn't see it from down on the river, which was about thirty feet below, because of the foliage.

I had a bullfrog croak I could do through a microphone that sounded fairly convincing. Through our PA, it sounded like a forty-foot bullfrog. So we'd wait for the canoers to get right underneath us, then I'd open up with the bullfrog. We'd have them diving out of the canoes.

"Plungin' like stones from a sling-shot on Mars"

WEIR: We had those feedback scenarios like you hear in "Caution" [on *Anthem of the Sun*], where everybody just opens fire with all the electronic weirdness at our disposal. We'd wait 'til a canoe got right underneath us and then, "Ready, aim,

FIRE!" We'd blast them with cosmic weirdness of a hellacious sort.

"But the heat came round and
busted me
For smilin' on a cloudy day"

WEIR: The charge was assault on an officer. They wouldn't have busted me, but after I did it I had to go out to the street and just kind of sit there and look at him and grin.

They beat me around a little bit at the station. They were not long on patience with hippies in the Haight-Ashbury precinct.

I beat the rap, though. They had nothing on me.

"Looking at you looking at me"

HERBIE GREENE

"OH, IT TALKS, DOES IT?"

96

HERB CAEN [San Francisco *Chronicle* columnist, March 18, 1969]: At the Hilton end of the Black and White Ball, the Grateful Dead, the pioneer S.F. rock group, was making a tremendous racket. . . . After the gig, Jerry Garcia was depressed. "We sounded terrible," he lamented, rubbing his thick, black beard. "Couldn't get the feel of the room. It was like playing in a cocktail lounge. We wanted to do a good job tonight— this is our hometown, after all—but we've played better on the road after five nights of no sleep. Too bad. But say, did you see all those people out on the floor dancing? Having fun? That part was fun. I wish the kids at the Fillmore who never dance could have seen that."

. . . As Garcia walked away, a society matron followed him with her eyes and said, "Oh, it talks, does it?" Yeah, it talks. "What in the world do you find to SAY to people like that?" she asked. I couldn't find anything to say to her, so I left.

"You ain't gonna learn what you
don't want to know"

GARCIA: That part of America that fears things, that can be made to be scared, reacted so badly to the Haight scene. Culturally, it was sort of a bright little thing. It just meant a little more freedom. Then all of a sudden, CLANG—the straight people's fear of drugs and the unknown created that suppression that came down so heavily. The backlash may ultimately have had more real effect than the thing itself.

LESH: We were too proud of it. . . . Did you ever flash that if you hadn't turned so many people on to pot the prices would be lower? [*Laughs*] It was kind of like that.

GARCIA: The people who were going to get something good out of that time have done all right. I know lots of people who are successfully doing something they invented back then, who never did drop back in. So it wasn't a total loss . . .

"Ran into a rainstorm . . ."

GARCIA: Woodstock was . . . two distinct experiences: the weekend itself, just like a person in the audience; and the experience of playing there, which for the Grateful Dead was really horrible.

For some reason or other we didn't trust the PA they had there that everybody else was using. So there was this long, long delay before we got to play, because there was no PA. Maybe four, five hours . . . interminable. I was high, of course—we were all getting high there.

HART: There were a lot of bad drugs going around that day, and everybody was doing one thing or another all day. By the time we got to play, everybody was all tweaked out in some way, shape, or form.

LESH: We were all high on Czechoslovakian acid—salmon pink, speckled tablets made of crystal that had been synthesized in Czechoslovakia by people who had been run out of town by the Russians in '68. The tanks came in and the acid left town. . . .

Paul Kantner and Bill Laudner, who was the ace equipment man for the Airplane, got caught trying to put this Czechoslovakian acid in the orange juice supply for the entire *back*SSS-STAAAAGE. They got caught that time, but it was everywhere. Everybody was doing everything. . . .

HART: Paul Kantner was at work for a better tomorrow—Paul's way.

GARCIA: We went out on the stage, which was *packed* with people. It was getting to be very, um, *wired* out there. It was raining, of course. Everything was conductive in some weird way. It looked like there were balls of electricity bouncing across the stage and jumping on my guitar. I'd get these incredible shocks—didn't have any-

KREUTZMANN, LESH, WEIR, AND GARCIA AT 710 ASHBURY STREET IN SAN FRANCISCO, 1966 OVERLEAF: TOMPKINS SQUARE PARK, NEW YORK CITY, JUNE 1967

FROM LEFT: LESH, GARCIA, ROSIE McGEE, LAIRD GRANT, KREUTZMANN, WEIR, TANGERINE, PIGPEN, MANAGERS ROCK SCULLY (STANDING), AND DANNY RIFKIN

thing to do with touching a microphone or being grounded in any of the normal ways.

WEIR: Every time I touched my guitar I got a shock. And if I made the mistake—which I did once and only once—of touching my guitar and microphone at the same time, that sent me flying about ten feet in the air, back against my amp stack. There was a big blue spark, and I had a fat lip afterwards.

LESH: They said they had a fifty-foot pipe sunk into the ground, but Bear lifted the ground to save our lives. It made the sound noisy as hell, but . . . Weir was talking about getting burned lips? He would have been dead.

ROCK SCULLY: They had set up this huge screen behind the band; the wind picked up and the screen became like a giant sail and the stage started to slide downhill! The band had to scramble and rip holes in this $10,000 screen with knives. Too much was going on. . . .

GARCIA: The stage was like twenty feet high. The light towers were these colossal things, maybe a hundred feet from the stage in several directions, and very tall. The lights were super-hot, giganto spotlights. So there was this kind of bug-on-a-microscope sensation, of being pinned by these spotlights—and knowing there were 300,000 people out there but not being able to see *anybody* because of the darkness and the blinding light. It was nightmarish beyond belief.

We tried to play our little music [*laughs*] in the midst of this incredible confusion. People were screaming, all this weird stuff was going on . . . announcements about "This acid is poison, it has strychnine in it and people are dying"—all this bad news pouring out constantly.

LESH: It was hilarious. The biggest crowd of all time, and the PA goes off for the Grateful Dead. And we were ready to blow their heads off. We were high on acid; we were ready to really lay it down.

> "Would you hear my voice
> Come through the music?"

LESH: Right in the middle of "Lovelight," these radio voices started coming out of my amplifier.

GARCIA: All the CB stuff the cops were using to communicate were leaking into the amplifiers, because of the unshielded pickups on the guitars and stuff.

LESH: When I saw that incident in the movie *Spinal Tap*, I almost shit in my pants. Art imitates life.

GARCIA: So there's these mystery voices pouring out of the amplifiers, electricity flashing around and giving you these terrible jolts . . . People were leaning across my amplifiers and saying stuff like, "The stage is collapsing! The stage is collapsing!" That was the ambience we tried to play in . . . It came off horribly. It was just awful. That part I'd just as soon forget.

But the rest of it was great fun. We had a swell time above and beyond that . . . wandering around, flashing on this enormous number of people. The *eventness* of it was very apparent even there, as though history was looking at it. I felt like it was crowded with invisible time travelers from the future.

LESH: We choppered out, and then we drove from the hotel to the airport to fly to New York. I was in a car with TC and I don't remember who else. The weather was blowing up again—the

"WE WERE THE FIRST WEIRD PEOPLE A LOT OF PLACES EVER SAW."—JERRY GARCIA

storms were lining up. . . . We got the great bolt—absolutely perfect timing, just the right distance—the voice of God. The thunder was absolutely perfect. And TC said, "Now *that's* the PA we need!"

When we got to New York City, we watched Crosby, Stills and Nash and the Jefferson Airplane on TV. . . . Grace was saying, "What's the matter with these people? All Walter Cronkite can talk about is garbage!" That was their coverage. That was their idea of what the Woodstock festival was all about: garbage. How 500,000 people can turn into a city in five days, and the result is garbage. Well, that's what your brain makes of it. Garbage in, garbage out, Walter!

"Steal your face right off your head"

LESH: We had to follow Miles Davis, three nights in a row, at the Fillmore West [September 1970]. I don't want to hear anybody snivel about following anybody else, because we got the *one*. Made me feel so dumb.

It was cold-blooded murder. Miles had his *Bitches Brew* band, a hot fucking band, and they played some stuff! Billy and Mickey and I were on stage for sure—I think everybody in our band was on stage, digging it and trying to keep up with the music. It was some dense stuff.

Then we had to *follow* these guys. It wasn't exactly stage fright I felt; it was like, How am I going to play this stuff after hearing that? I'd much rather listen to more! [*Laughs*]

KREUTZMANN: I was embarrassed. We should have opened for *him*, for God's sake!

LESH: I thought, What am I doing here? Why aren't I at home digesting what I just heard?

KREUTZMANN: We played really free and loose, because I couldn't get Miles out of my head. It had a tremendous effect on what we played that night.

BILL GRAHAM: Booking Miles Davis and the Dead was like telling a kid, "I know you want ice cream, but you've got to eat the meat first." The audience had no choice—there was Miles Davis, and they had to eat that. People would say, "Aw, we've got to sit through *this*?" And I'd stand at the side of the stage and *watch the conversion*.

"Might as well travel the elegant way"

GARCIA: We had a lot of people we wanted to take to Europe. . . . You don't make money playing England, so we needed to record an album there to pay the bills.

WEIR: *Europe '72* was the answer to a whole lot of questions, like how the hell are we gonna be able to afford to take the entire staff and crew on a European vacation. . . . Through a great deal of hassling and haggling, it actually came to pass. . . . And lo and behold, the album paid for the tour—which I thought was a nice way to do it.

GARCIA: Everything has many uses . . .

◆　　◆　　◆

In 1970 and 1971, the Dead toured with the New Riders of the Purple Sage, a country and bluegrass band featuring old Palo Alto cohorts David Nelson and John "Marmaduke" Dawson (who also wrote most of their material) on guitars. Garcia played pedal steel and banjo, and their early rhythm section consisted of Lesh and Hart. Dave Torbert, later of Kingfish, soon came in on bass, and ex-Jefferson Airplane drummer Spencer Dryden became the NRPS drummer in 1971.

Several of the Dead's tours in 1970 were billed as "An Evening with the Grateful Dead and the New Riders of the Purple Sage," and the Dead threw in acoustic sets to kick off the shows. It all added up to an American music review, including bluegrass, country, and gospel standards, Pigpen's all-too-rare solo blues numbers, jug band chestnuts like "Monkey and the Engineer," "Wake Up Little Susie," folk tunes, and the rapidly developing Grateful Dead originals from *Workingman's Dead* and *American Beauty*.

With the addition of Canadian steelman

104

MIT, MAY 7, 1970, DURING THE STUDENT STRIKE IN PROTEST OF THE KENT STATE KILLINGS

Buddy Cage in late 1971, the New Riders became a self-contained band and began to tour and record independently of the Dead, although the two bands remained close and shared many stages over the next several years.

"Balls of lightning roll along"

BARLOW: They played Folsom Field in Boulder at the height of the thunderstorm season [September 3, 1972], and one of those really majestic cumulo-nimbi squatted on Boulder right in the middle of the concert. After unleashing a torrent of hail borne on really wild winds, it started to hit everything with lightning.

The PA system had more watts than you could produce with a Waukesha engine, and it was isolated from the ground and insulated by Astroturf. Pretty soon, St. Elmo's fire began to gather on the scaffolding—and the band continued to play.

There was a very low neoprene roof over the area of the stage where the band was, and it was filling up with water. We had to cut slits in it or it would probably have brought twelve or thirteen tons down at once and squished everybody; in their moment of near-electrocution they would have been crushed by water.

A couple of us tied knives onto the ends of sticks and stood on boxes to cut the roof, trying to make sure the water didn't come down onto the amplifiers. Then there was water all over the stage, three to six inches depending on where you were.

Some guy—some really remarkable guy—came dashing up the stairs, barefoot, plugged in a Skilsaw, and started cutting square holes in the floor of the stage to let the water drain. He was *in* the water, barefoot, while everyone else was up on boxes.

The band played through all of this, oblivious. Nobody got electrocuted; nobody made that good connection.

THE DEAD WITH NEW SINGER DONNA GODCHAUX (AND WITHOUT PIGPEN, WHO WAS ILL) JUST BEFORE THE EUROPE '72 TOUR

MARY ANN MAYER

"If you've got a dollar, boys
Lay it on the line"

WEIR: We don't use the safe side of technology—we use the experimental side. We'll try the prototype of any new thing that comes out, and it works about half the time, so technology is sort of an albatross for us. But it's fun when it works.

DAN HEALY [sound engineer]: Every one of us has had many ideas—"This is it!"—and spent a lot of time and energy, then had it go *pfffft*.

At Stanford [February 9, 1973], when we were debuting the first version of the big '74 sound system, we rebuilt all these Electro-Voice tweeters and spent maybe twenty thousand dollars on amps, crossovers, and stuff. In the first two seconds of the first song, every single one of those brand-new tweeters got smoked. About eighty of 'em, wiped out. We'd gone through all these changes to put in protection devices, and they blew long after the speakers were gone. And we

had maybe a dozen spares . . . We opened up the crossovers and faked it the rest of the night.

HEALY: The 1974 sound system had fifty-five 600-watt power amplifiers, and separate speaker systems for each instrument and the vocals. Since no two sounds went through any one speaker, the sound was staggeringly clean—and it could be amazingly loud.

In those days we could go into a hall three days before a gig and set up a stage, check the place out . . . It's no longer practical to have two stages and three semis full of instruments, amps, and speakers—and it's no longer necessary. The sound system we have now is more efficient than the '74 "Wall of Sound."

"Too much of anything is just
enough"

JIM FURMAN: I was kind of an electronics maintenance person, the emergency troubleshooter for

107

MARY ANN MAYER

the sound system. We were going to be kind of stuck out in the country at Watkins Glen [September 27–28, 1973] with a very elaborate system, and if it blew up I was supposed to fix it as best I could.

At that time the Dead's PA was built heavily around McIntosh 2300 power amps, and they decided to add five more for that performance. Watkins Glen is right near Binghamton, New York, where the McIntosh factory is. No store had five 2300s in stock, so I was given a helicopter and about six thousand dollars in cash with instructions to come back with five of them.

I contacted a dealer in Binghamton who said the McIntosh factory was shut down for two weeks for their annual vacation. This guy knew the president of McIntosh, though, and he called him up and made a special arrangement.

108

THE DEAD AND THE NEW RIDERS, CIRCA 1970. (*LEFT TO RIGHT*): GARCIA, DAVID NELSON, DAVE TORBERT, PIGPEN, WEIR, HART, JOHN DAWSON, LESH, KREUTZMANN.

HERBIE GREENE

PETER SIMON

NEW RIDERS OF THE PURPLE SAGE, MAY 1970. DAVID NELSON AND JERRY GARCIA.

The helicopter took me from backstage at Watkins Glen—it was impossible to drive out, because all the roads were clogged; this was bigger than Woodstock, around 600,000 people—to the Binghamton airport. I took a cab downtown, and this dealer got the president of McIntosh, who was just about to take off on vacation with his wife and kids. He picked me up in his station wagon I had to sit with the kids in the back—drove to the factory, opened it up, and took five units out, went back to the store and counted out the cash. I was just wearing a T-shirt and shorts, because it was really hot, so I had the cash rolled up in my shirt. Then the guy who owned the store called the Binghamton Police Department, explained the situation, and got special permission for the helicopter to land right in the middle of downtown to pick me and the amps up.

"God damn, well I declare! Have you seen the like?"

"I would love to play the pedal steel guitar, if I had another lifetime in which to play it. It's really a weird instrument. . . . It's crippling if you think of it as some sort of mutated guitar; you have to erase the guitar entirely from your thinking." —JERRY GARCIA

Canadian Customs got the Grateful Dead coming and going in the fall of 1977. It began when a suspicious substance was discovered in somebody's luggage.

WEIR: I had this little baggie full of bee pollen, which is a really wonderful food—especially if you're a distance runner. They wanted to know

ON THE BOZO BUS DURING THE EUROPE '72 TOUR. WEIR AND FRANKIE, WITH STEVE PARISH (*LEFT*) ELEVATING AN ARTIFICIAL DIGIT

what it was, and I told them, "Just smell it, that's all I want you to do. Smell it and you'll know it's bee pollen. There's *nothing else on earth* that could possibly smell like bee pollen."

They wouldn't smell it. They put it through all their computers, and they strip-searched us and all that kind of, uh, garbage. Then we got in [to Canada].

We played the gig in Toronto [Seneca College Field House, November 2, 1977], and it was a real hot one. Then coming back out of Canada they busted us again for the same damn thing: bee pollen.

◆   ◆   ◆

"Let's see with our hearts . . ."

GARCIA: Playing in Egypt [August 14–16, 1978] was a fantasy that existed for a long time. The Mideast is so touchy politically that we never thought it would be possible, but a friend of ours visited Egypt and told us it was great—"and

"DRUMMING IS A PHYSICAL RELEASE FOR ME. WHEN I WAS A KID, I'D HAVE FIGHTS WITH MY PARENTS AND THEN GO TO MY ROOM AND BEAT MY DRUMS FOR HOURS."—BILL KREUTZMANN

there's an ideal place to play, right by the pyramids."

HART: We could think of no one better to get us there than Bill Graham. We wanted Bill to buy a good PA so we could use it, and we wanted some help finding more acoustically appropriate places to play.

Phil and I decided it was time to take our agenda to Bill, so we made placards that said *BETTER SOUND, MORE TRIPS, EGYPT OR BUST*, and we went to Bill's house. It happened to be around eleven o'clock at night, so we shined flashlights in his windows. He came out—"What's happening? What's going on?!"

"Okay, Graham, back in the house! We're gonna talk business!" We went inside, took his

112

LESH AND BILL GRAHAM BACKSTAGE AT THE BAY AREA MUSIC AWARDS, MARCH 1980. PHIL AGREED TO ACCEPT HIS BEST BASS PLAYER "BAMMIE" (HIS SECOND IN THE THREE-YEAR HISTORY OF THE HONOR) IN PERSON IF THEY PROMISED NOT TO GIVE IT TO HIM ANYMORE.

RICHARD McCAFFREY

phones off the hook, and presented our "demands." We talked until dawn.

Bill didn't think we should go to the Middle East, because there was a war going on over there and somebody might get hurt. I told him, "That's why we *have* to go there. This is a way we can do something." Bill didn't see it that way; he thought it was dangerous.

So we did it ourselves.

"Blues for Allah
In 'sh'Allah"

HART: This would be a real test of the power of the music, to play in a place where nobody had any expectations of us and we didn't have the

NEW YEAR'S DAY, 1973. WEIR AND BILL GRAHAM AT WEIR'S PLACE IN THE EARLY MORNING HOURS

ANDY LEONARD

113

safety net of conditioned responses. We weren't there on our terms, nor on the audience's terms. We were *all* there on the desert's terms—and the desert had never seen amplified Western music, not to mention the Grateful Dead.

GARCIA: We began to make contact with the diplomatic world—the private sector of the diplomatic circle, though, rather than the State Department. We put together our own diplomatic mission, in effect.

We set the gigs up as a benefit, with part of the proceeds going to Mrs. Sadat's favorite charity and part to the Department of Antiquities in Cairo. So it worked out great.

LESH: . . .We went to see a most remarkable person, Dr. Moishe Saad-ed-Din, who I believe was the Egyptian deputy minister of culture. Poet, writer, friend of Lawrence Durrell's, former head of the secret police, all in one person. The terms in which he grasped it! . . .

We talked about how we wouldn't make any money except from a record of the performances—and the Egyptians would get a piece of that, too—so there should be no feeling of "Here come the white boys to rip us off again."

HART: How do you describe "trips" to an Egyptian? The journey was something we took very seriously. It wasn't a "whim," as some have described it. You don't spend $500,000 on a whim. This was something we'd wanted to do for years. Without sounding too mystical, I'd say we felt *drawn* there.

LESH: About fifteen minutes into the conversation Dr. Saad-ed-Din turned to me and said, "Have you ever played any place outside the U.S.?"

I said, "We've played in Europe," and he said, "Have you found that your music changes when you play in different places?"

I said, "Precisely, and that's why we want to play at the pyramids," and he said, "I thought so." That changed it in their eyes from somebody jacking off to somebody meaning business. It went through various government officials after that, but from that moment on it was essentially a fait accompli.

HART: After it was all put together and we got

to Egypt safely, Bill Graham decided maybe it wasn't so dangerous after all and came on over—as our guest, not as the producer. I've never seen Bill higher.

LESH: I like Bill better as a pleasure cruiser. When he can relax and have fun, he's the best.

HARRY POPICK [monitor mixer]: It took an awful long time to set up, because it was so brutally hot that we could only work at night—and even then it didn't cool down very much. I'd go to move speaker cabinets and find them melted to each other.

The kids there had never seen Frisbees. We had some in the equipment boxes, and when we started throwing them around, the kids were amazed. It was a great feeling, showing half a dozen kids how a Frisbee works and throwing it around with them. I wish we'd had more of them to give away.

> "Ain't a place a man can hide . . .
> Will keep him from the sun . . ."

POPICK: It took me three days to get ice. We had requested it in advance, but I don't think the Egyptians knew what we were going to do with it.

WEIR: They don't drink much beer in the Islamic countries, so they only have it for the tourists. They don't really know what to do with it—like put it on ice, for instance.

POPICK: I got one of the cab drivers we'd hired for the week to drive me into Cairo. We rode around until I saw some buckets. I stopped the driver and pointed at them—[*counting on his fingers*] "three, four, five!"—and he said, "Okay," and parked. He said he'd be right back and vanished down an alley.

I sat there looking around and wondering what was going on for about fifteen minutes. Then he came back with five or six buckets. On the way back to the pyramids, we stopped at a store for beer. I knew the word for that . . .

WEIR: There is one government-run brewery, and you can get one brand of beer in Egypt. It's called Stella Beer. They import some beer, but it's real hard to find.

118

POPICK: We got cases and cases of beer, and we finally got some ice. The driver knew what we wanted to do: fill the buckets with ice and make the beer cold!

Once we got all the ice distributed and everything was chilling, people started hanging around the buckets the way they would around a fire, with their hands out to feel the coolness. I'm sure they weren't aware they were doing it.

◆ ◆ ◆

WEIR: At the beginning of the show the Deadheads would come to the front of the stage the way they always do. The Egyptians took their seats and waited for the concert to start. After the show got going, the Egyptians got up and started moving closer, and they crowded the Deadheads out. By the end of the concert each night, the complexion of the audience had changed. It was considerably darker, and the hair was a lot curlier. . . .

HART: We were up for Egypt, of course, and the magic did happen. But it didn't happen in an avalanche. It was more subtle. There were technical difficulties, and Kreutzmann had a broken hand. . . . We went into the concerts not running on all cylinders.

"I was having a high time . . ."

BILL GRAHAM: The Nubians were playing before the Dead, in this wonderful theater under the Sphinx and the Great Pyramid. All of a sudden there was a little sound, a light melody like a bird. Jerry was standing behind his amplifier, playing along with these Egyptian rhythms. Then I heard Lesh, and the rest of the band came in . . .

HART: This began the segue into the Grateful Dead set. Here we were, together, playing this new music created especially for the moment!

These were people who didn't know "Sugaree" and "Truckin'," so it came down to how the music made them feel. We had only sound—and the

sounds of the words, not their literal meanings—to work with.

KREUTZMANN: Egypt reaffirmed my belief in playing music for people. Even though they didn't understand the words, they were all out there dancing in their robes. . . . It was very far out to go to a country where they've never heard our music.

"Sometimes when the night is dyin'
I take me out and I wander around"

GRAHAM: It was one of the two or three public highs I've ever had.

After the first show Mickey took me out horse riding in the middle of the night, along with some other people. I almost fell off the damn horse when Omar [the guide] whipped it. He kept on saying, "Ride the body! Relax! Ride the body!" And I finally relaxed.

It felt like Errol Flynn and Douglas Fairbanks riding off into the desert. Five miles out, in the middle of nowhere, we came to a tent. A waiter came out and said, "Stella—or Seven-Up?"

119

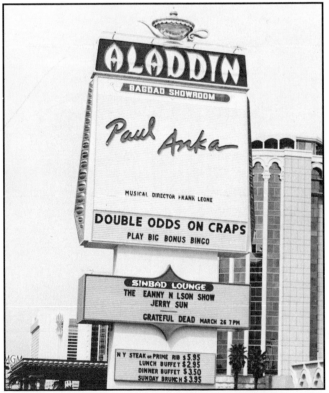

LAS VEGAS, MARCH 1983.

DAVID GANS

It was a full moon, and we could see the Sphinx and the Great Pyramid back where we'd come from. Omar said, "In about twenty minutes you should face that way," pointing to the east. And at twenty-one minutes after five, this crimson ball of fire came up out of the sand. And for the first time in my life, as far as I could see, there was nothing. Just sand.

"Peals of fragile thunder keeping time"

GRAHAM: The Nubians played this twelve-beat chant, and by the third night I had learned the pattern of the handclaps. For the first time in my *life* I left the stage, walked out in front, and danced. I was wearing a robe and headpiece and I sweated like a pig—and had a wonderful time.

After the show, at four o'clock in the morning, I rented sixty-four camels and horses and took the entire group back out to that tent. We had breakfast and watched the sunrise, Ken Kesey and Bill Walton had camel races, Garcia was riding around. . . . We had a ball.

WEIR: I think Madame Sadat saw to it that everybody in Egypt was going to love the Grateful Dead, and by God, they did. And surprisingly quickly after we got back, we got reports and documents showing what had been done with the funds we raised. Madame Sadat's children's charity benefited, and a lot of the money went to build soccer fields for kids in the little villages along the Nile.

GARCIA: We got good marks. And the Egyptians loved hippies.

◆　　◆　　◆

WEIR AND HART WITH PREMIER REGGAE DRUMMER SLY DUNBAR AT THE JAMAICA WORLD MUSIC FESTIVAL IN MONTEGO BAY, NOVEMBER 1982

PETER SIMON

DAVID GANS

WEIR: I like what happens when this band gets force-fed unusual circumstances.

We played at the Milky Way club in Amsterdam on the '81 Europe tour [October 15–16] using borrowed and rented equipment.

LESH: We'd gotten cancelled in the south of France after selling sixty-nine tickets in one location and zero in the other. Somebody had made the mistake of booking a rock concert after the end of the vacation season, and everybody'd gone back to Paris.

Nobody wanted to sit around for three days. . . . Somebody said, "Let's go to Amsterdam and play," and everybody said, "*Yeaaahhhh! Amsterdam!*" Rock [Scully] knows a lot of people there, so he talked to all the right people and set it up.

POPICK: All the band's stuff was en route to the next regular gig, except the cymbals and a few other things, and a bit of test equipment I brought along.

Healy and I took a look at the club's sound system a day or so before the first show, and we fixed enough discrepancies that when the band started playing we were much closer to being balanced. We had to mess around with the whole thing for a while, but it was a lot of fun.

LESH: I went to Copenhagen to hear the Vienna Philharmonic, conducted by Leonard Bernstein, performing Brahms' Fourth Symphony, and then I caught up with the band in Amsterdam.

I was the only one who brought an instrument. The other guys were playing borrowed guitars, and everybody was playing borrowed amplifiers. . . .

WEIR: I was playing an imitation Telecaster through a Twin Reverb, and I think Brent played a really funky Fender Rhodes—definitely not our usual sound. We played reasonably well, but we didn't last long because of the heat.

POPICK: It was *staggeringly* hot! There must have been many, many more people than there were supposed to be. The band had a sound that I had never heard before. It was very, very nice.

WEIR: We did "Lovelight" for the first time in a long time, and we also played "Gloria." Everybody got real loose.

LESH: "Lovelight" just kind of happened—I

OVERLEAF: AFTER THE DEAD'S SET AT THE US FESTIVAL, KREUTZMANN, WEIR, AND HART SAT IN THE WATER AND MET THE PRESS.

LYNN GOLDSMITH

GARCIA LEAVES THE US FESTIVAL SITE, SEPTEMBER 5, 1982.

found myself playing it, and it was like a great orgasm.

WEIR: I think everybody had fun just being in a different environment.

We'd never experienced anything like the Us Festival [September 5, 1982], either. It was as foreign as going to Egypt to us, to get up and play at nine in the morning—much less to a crowd that wasn't a hundred percent Deadheads. Hell, it put us into emergency mode—"Here are all these strange faces and this is a weird time to be playing"—and the only way for us to deal with it was to lean into it.

LESH [onstage at the Us Festival just before the band began their Sunday morning set]: So, this is the Us Festival, right? Well, how are *we* feeling this morning? Well, settle down and spread, 'cause it's time for breakfast in bed with the Grateful Dead!

WEIR: There were a lot of equipment breakdowns in the first part of the show, but we pulled it together. We were all busy waking up, our equipment was busy waking up, the crew was busy waking up—and the crowd was busy waking up. By the time we got rolling, we just kept rolling until they were ready to get the hooks and drag us off the stage. We were having fun, in the most absurd—at least by our standards—circumstances.

HART: We were the breakfast show!

WEIR: That was to our advantage, because they got us out of bed and put us on the stage before we had a chance to get cold feet about playing in that heat.

CHAPTER

9
Pigpen

TALK ABOUT YOUR PLENTY, TALK ABOUT YOUR ILLS

"Pigpen was our showpiece, and he did something nobody else is going to get close to. He was so good at what he did! He was one ugly guy, but he was so bodacious about his delivery." —BOB WEIR

"If I could have one wish in the world, it would be that Pigpen could still be with us. I think it's safe to say we *all* miss Pigpen."

—Phil Lesh

A hard-drinking, acid-shunning blues harmonica player might have seemed incongruous amidst the multicolored madness of the Acid Test, but Ron "Pigpen" McKernan made the kind of direct, visceral human contact that made LSD seem like the long way around.

It's hard to imagine how much distance the Grateful Dead could cover in the forty-five minutes or so from "Dark Star" to "Lovelight," but they knew how to get all the way outside and Pigpen knew how to get all the way inside. The band was just as electrifying in service of Pig's musky muse as it was in the cerebral universes of free-form improvisation.

Playing behind Pigpen wasn't the usual vamp-until-ready R&B review routine. He stood out front and poured himself into his words while the band kept the groove moving behind him. On a particularly hot night they could follow him so closely you couldn't tell whether he was leading the band or the music was driving him.

The son of an R&B disc jockey, Pigpen got hip to down-and-dirty blues at an early and susceptible age. He had the kind of unfortunate face and physique that built character and invariably encased a tender heart and a generous soul. Because he was a hard-looking man, people took him for a hard man, but Pig just nurtured his gifts and let the faint of heart think what they thought.

His heroes were Lightnin' Hopkins, John Lee Hooker, Bobby "Blue" Bland, Junior Parker, Little Walter. He made Otis Redding's "Hard to Handle" his own without disturbing Otis's patent, and he delivered James Brown's "It's a Man's World" with authority, too. What the hell did he need acid for? If everywhere the Dead played was church, Pigpen was a holy roller of the heart.

◆　　◆　　◆

HART: When I first saw the Grateful Dead it was a blues band. Pigpen played blues harp, and he was the musician in the group. It was Pig and the boys back then.

MARY ANN MAYER

128

LESH: When the band got going, I elected myself to be the guy who made sure Pigpen got up for practice every day. First of all, I made sure he put the telephone by his shoulder when he went to sleep at night, because otherwise he wouldn't hear it ringing in the morning and he wouldn't get up.

He was living in Palo Alto with his folks. Every day, seven days a week, we'd go over there at nine or ten o'clock in the morning and the other guys would wait in Jerry's Corvair while I went and got Pig. Most of the time I just knocked on the window, but sometimes I had to crawl through and physically wake him up.

He'd crawl out the window so he wouldn't disturb anybody inside, and he'd tuck his bottle of Southern Comfort into his pants as we walked to the car.

◆   ◆   ◆

STEVE O'SHEA [deejay of KFRC, introducing the band members in a 1966 interview]: Pigpen—what a horrible name!

PIGPEN: It's not my fault—Jerry gave it to me.

O'SHEA: I understand there's a Pigpen T-shirt. Does that mean you've arrived and you're a star now?

PIGPEN: Well, it's their fault over there—the fan club.

WEIR: We brought one for you. It's fluorescent, no less.

O'SHEA: Oh, is that lovely. . . . Thank you. I'll wear that to—well, I'll figure out somewhere to wear that.

TC: Pigpen was wonderful. There was an incredible dichotomy between the person and the image, and sometimes the person would play off the image.

HART: He looked hard, but he was a soft man. He had to look tough because he was so gentle that he'd get stepped on.

◆   ◆   ◆

The Dead played acoustic sets off and on throughout 1970, mixing up the material from

BARON WOLMAN

HERBIE GREENE

Workingman's Dead and *American Beauty* with some country and bluegrass standards and a couple of their old jug band tunes. Pigpen threw in some piano and a harp lick here and there, and the band played with him on "Operator." And every so often he'd step out there all by his lonesome and do one, an example of which (Fillmore East, February 13, 1970) was included on *Bear's Choice.*

ROCK SCULLY: We'd been pushing him for years, and finally he got loose enough and comfortable enough to go out and do it. He went out on the stage and sat down in a chair and played bottleneck guitar. He had a honey in the crowd, and he sang "Katie Mae" for her.

GARCIA: Pigpen influenced a lot of what we were doing just because of who he was. The music had to be structured within his ability; if we came up with anything that was too complicated for him, he'd lay out.

HART: He played hard, but he played the blues—shuffle stuff. That was his medium. He *was* the blues.

LESH: He was a soloist with his voice and his harp and his personality, but he wasn't really much of an organ player. He'd play little parts in "The Other One," which was always helpful for the texture, but when we started getting into more extended spaces, he would lay out—which was for the best, I guess. We wanted him to be there with us, because he really was one of us, but he would lay out.

Rather than try and describe what Pigpen did, I'd say you should listen to him. The best thing I could recommend is a tape from Princeton University in 1971 [April 19]. That "Good Lovin' " is the quintessential Pigpen: The tape will explain it all.

I was goin' down the street one day
Right after me and my old lady got in a fight
I see this dude on the corner
He said, "Say, man, you look like you kinda
    lonesome."
I said, "Yeah, well, me and my old lady

We had kind of a fallin' out, you
     understand."
He said, "Well, hey, listen—
I just got into bidness."
I said, "You just got into bidness?
Jack, what you talkin' about, bidness?"
He say, "I'm in commercial merchandise,"
     he says.
I say, "What kind of merchandise you got?"
He say, "Whatchoo want?"
Well, I said, "You got any dope?
Are you in the automobile bidness?
Do you fix refrigerators?
Do you fix windows?
Are you a plumber?"
He said, "No, man. I got myself a Cadillac."
I said, "Oh, yeah?"
He say, "What seem to be your trouble?"
I said, "Well, you know, me and my old
     lady,
We just had a little falling out."
He said, "Oh, that's it, huh?"
He say, "Well, listen:
I got about anything you want."

MARY ANN MAYER

He say, uh,
"How much money you got in yo' pocket?"
And I tell him, "Well, I got about a dollar
     and a quarter."
He kinda step back a taste and say,
"Dollar and a quarter?
Wait a minute now!
You can't buy much for a dollar and a
     quarter!"
I said, "I don't want much—
I just want a little bit."
He said, "Well, maybe I can fix you up."
This fella slow down
And a-turn around . . .
Slow down and a-turn around
Scratch his head just a little bit
He say,
"I got a i-DEEEEEEA!!!"
And he said,
"I got the impression that you ain't lookin'
     for nothin' high class,
Just somethin' to take care of yo' natch'ral
     needs."

He say, "Look down on the corner. See that
     girl?"
I said, "What girl?"
He said, "The big one!"
"That a GIRL? I thought that was the
     Brooklyn Bridge."
He say, "How much you got?"
I say, "A dollar and a quarter."
"SOLD! The Brooklyn Bridge!"

So I went down and said,
"The man down the street said I can come
     home witchoo."
She said, "It's all right now, Daddy,
Show me what you can do."
And don't you know, now, people,
She treated me nice and kind.
She made me
She made me think
She sure did treat me fine
For a buck and a quarter
What more do you want?
For a buck and a quarter!

BOB SEIDEMANN

HERBIE CREENE

HERBIE GREENE

JIM MARSHALL

What more do you want?
Things get goin'
They don't be slowin'
Cooked on this side
Say now, Mama, won't you roll on over
Let me jump on your wagon and ride
Let me jump on your wagon and ride, now
    baby
Let me jump on your wagon and ride
Let me jump on your wagon and ride, now
    Mama
Jump on your wagon and ride
That's all I need
A little bit of love
A little bit of love in my soul
And a whole other kind of places
And a whole other kind of taste-es
That's all I need
That's all I got to git, now
All right!

[Instrumental]

Cost me a buck and a quarter
For my pony ride
Twenty more dollars

When the doctor was by my side
He's got that needle
Sayin' "Brother, are you in trouble,
Thinkin' that was the way to go."
She may have been fun
But it wasn't no fun later on
No it wasn't
Went around
All over town
Went around
Over town
Wond'rin' what my lady was up to now
Just a-wond'rin' what she's doin'
While I'm on the prowl
Axed my doctor what to do
He said, "Now, son,
I know just exactly what's wrong with you.
You need a little bit of lovin'
Good ol' love
Nothin' on the side
Need a love, a good ol' love
Don't blow your pride."
I want to tell you now
After I was feelin' so bad
And I had all them troubles

132

LEFT TO RIGHT: KREUTZMANN, GODCHAUX, GARCIA, WEIR, PIGPEN, LESH, FALL 1971

I want to tell you jus' about what happened
Yes I do
Yes I do

—Excerpt from the "Good Lovin' "
rap, April 19, 1971

LESH: That was his peak. After that, his health started to decline.

HART: I don't think he was [unhappy]. He was just living the blues life, you know, singin' the blues and drinkin' whiskey. That's what all blues guys did. That went along with the blues. And it killed him.

GARCIA: We were prepared emotionally for Pigpen's death a year and a half before it happened, when he first went into serious illness. There was a week when everybody gave blood for him. . . . He was in really bad shape, and it looked like he was going to die. Then he recovered and slowly got himself back together.

Getting that ill straightened him out more than any talk from us ever did. He was really working at getting himself together, and he came back to work with the band for a while, but then he just snuck away. It was typical of him, the kind of person he was.

He didn't drink for the last year and a half, but his body was just shot, beyond the point where it could repair itself. It wasn't as though he went on some final bender and then killed himself. He was actually on the road to a new persona, a new self.

HART: Pigpen lived it and he believed it. He got caught in that web and he couldn't break out.

SCULLY: We found out later he had what is called terminal liver, and even though he didn't drink for over a year, it was too late. He made the Hollywood Bowl concert [June 17, 1972], but that was the last one. He looked just terrible. He had developed pneumonia and was just in terrible shape.

He came to the Dead office maybe twelve hours before he died. He came in and said the doctors didn't see any reason why he shouldn't go back to work with the band. We were overjoyed. We were about to go into the studio to record, and we thought he was going to be with us, so it was a terrible shock when we were told his body had been found. He died late Tuesday night [March 6, 1973] or early Wednesday morning, right after he told us he was coming back to us.

We never figured out whether or not he knew all along that he was dying and just didn't want to lay that on us.

GARCIA: Pigpen's decline represented some kind of imminent change. He was more of a showman, more out there than the rest of us. We don't have that anymore.

I tend to think of the Grateful Dead's existence in terms of the Pigpen-as-center period and then the more self-sufficient, growing-out time that came when we got used to playing without him. It's not a question of better or worse—it's just different. Getting Keith [Godchaux], we became a different band.

see him standing
spread-legged
on the stage of the world
the boys prodding him
egging him on
he telling all he ever knew
or cared to know
mike hand cocked like
a boxer's
head thrown back
stale whiskey blues
many-peopled desolations
neon rainy streets
& wilderness of airports
thousands maybe millions
loved him
were fired instantly
into forty-five minutes of
midnight hour
but when he died
he was thin, sick, scared
alone

—From "He Was a Friend of Mine," Bobby Petersen's memorial to Pigpen, Mt. Hermon, California March 11, 1973

133

CHAPTER

10
Keyboards

LOOKING FOR FAMILIAR FACES

"We've lost a couple of players. . . . That piano bench seems to be something of a hot seat." —BOB WEIR

"One of the original members has gone to the Great Beyond—we think. Since then we've recruited a few other stooges . . . "

— Jerry Garcia

LESH: It was okay for Pigpen to lay out of the jams. He didn't mind, and we didn't mind. There was no ego problem there. I don't think he ever got pissed off when we wanted somebody who could play keyboards, because that wasn't really his forte.

TC had helped us with the prepared piano piece ["We Leave the Castle"] on *Anthem of the Sun,* and he joined the band in late 1968—as an addition, not to replace Pigpen.

TC: It was like a magic carpet that was there for me, and I would have been a fool not to step on it.

The whole time I was with the band I was plagued with problems of amplification. My dy-

namic range consisted of triple forte and double forte. Below that was inaudible, so finding a place for myself in the mix was difficult.

I wanted to be able to say something and stay out of their way. You can have all kinds of musical activity side by side as long as it's in prescribed areas of the audible spectrum. Mahler was a genius at that—he'd have six, seven, eight things going on that you could hear clearly.

LESH: TC never got over a certain stiffness. He couldn't *swing*—or at least he couldn't swing with us, at that time, and that was a problem. He only played with the band for a little over a year.

TC: Having the limited input I had with the Dead wasn't getting me off, and it wasn't getting them off, either. I had an offer to be the composer and musical director of *Tarot* [a music/theater project], which was moving to New York. The prospect of being a bigger fish in a smaller pond was one that I found inviting, so the Dead and I agreed amicably that I would be going on to something else.

My involvement with Scientology didn't help any. It made me a nonparticipant in the chemical

KEITH AT THE KEYS, LONDON 1972

sacraments of the time, and that offended Owsley greatly. I tried not to proselytize, but I'm sure there was a certain amount that I couldn't resist, and that must have rubbed some people the wrong way. *That* I regret.

WEIR: Garcia had done a session with Keith Godchaux, and he figured he could probably fill the keyboard spot. He brought Keith to the place where we were rehearsing in San Rafael, he auditioned, and everybody figured he'd do okay. We taught him the tunes, and he worked out fine for a while.

◆ ◆ ◆

Keith Godchaux grew up in Concord, California, the son of a sometime professional pianist/singer. Beginning at age five, he had five years of classical training. "It didn't stick," Godchaux told writer Jon Sievert in 1976. "I didn't have the temperament to pursue it." He did come out with

a certain amount of piano technique, although he said it "wasn't deep."

He kept playing the piano on his own, though, and at age fourteen joined a band. "I spent two years wearing dinner jackets and playing acoustic piano in country club bands and Dixieland groups."

By the time he was sixteen, Godchaux had acquired "a reputation" in the Concord area, and he began getting calls to put trios together for bar gigs. "I also did piano bar gigs and put trios together to back singers in various places around the Bay Area."

Most of those gigs consisted of playing "cocktail standards like 'Misty,' " Godchaux told Sievert, delivered "the way jazz musicians resentfully play a song that's popular—that frustrated space."

And why wasn't he playing rock and roll like other boys his age? "When other kids my age

MARY ANN MAYER

KEITH GODCHAUX (*FAR LEFT*) BEGAN REHEARSING WITH THE DEAD IN SEPTEMBER 1971. HE PLAYED HIS FIRST GIG IN MID-OCTOBER.

136

were going to dances and stuff, I was going to bars and playing." He was tired of that routine by the time he was old enough to drink. "For a pianist, a trio is fun because it gives you a lot of space," he said. "I just wasn't into it.

"That was only part of my life," he continued. "In the other half of my life I was looking for something real to get involved with—which wouldn't necessarily be music." A day job? Well, "I never could see working during the day, and nobody would hire me for anything, anyway."

As the jazz trio began "going in the Chick Corea direction," Godchaux found he "didn't really have any feeling for that type of music." He turned to the blues, big band jazz, Bill Evans— "the musicians the guys I was playing with were emulating." He spent a lot of time hanging out with these older players, listening to records and learning about the roots of jazz. "After gigs we'd go to somebody's house and listen to jazz until the sun came up. They dug turning me on to bebop and where it came from. So I understood *those* roots, but I never got taken on that kind of trip with rock and roll—and I never had the sense to take myself on it."

Rock continued to elude Keith until he met the woman who was to become his wife. Donna Jean Thatcher came to California from Muscle Shoals, Alabama, where she'd been a studio singer (her picture appears on the inside of the first *Boz Scaggs* album, which was recorded in Muscle Shoals).

DONNA AND KEITH GODCHAUX ON THE ROAD WITH THE DEAD, SPRING 1977

"She was well aware of the roots of rock and roll, and she gave me the flash," Godchaux recalled. "I started playing what I thought that flash was in the few remaining bar gigs that I had, but two months later I was completely burned out on that.

"Then I floated for about six months, and then I ended up playing with the Grateful Dead."

His improvisational background was in an entirely different style from the Grateful Dead's, but when the gig came his way in November 1971, Godchaux and his new bandmates found plenty of common musical ground on which to meet.

"I'm just now starting to learn about the type of music I'm playing now," he confessed in an interview during rehearsals for the Dead's June 1976 "comeback" tour. "Like I said, I never played rock and roll before I started playing with the Grateful Dead."

LESH: He was so brilliant at the beginning. That guy had it all; he could play anything. But after a certain point he didn't want to play.

WEIR: Keith really didn't like it here. He was bored with life in general, and he would freely tell anybody that. The darkness came upon him, and it pretty much took control. He was just not interested in living. It was reflected in his music and in everything else.

LESH: By '72, Donna had joined the band, too. That didn't help, either. You know how difficult it is having husband and wife in the same band?

GARCIA: It's tough to work with your old lady under any circumstances. . . .

Donna was great in the studio—she's got good ears—and she was able to sing in my band okay. When Donna and Keith were singing with me, the three of us had a nice blend. But with the Grateful Dead, she never really learned to hear herself on stage—or she was never positioned appropriately, or we never had a monitoring system that allowed her to hear herself clearly, I don't know. She had a hard time singing in key on stage.

WEIR: Keith played acoustic piano almost exclusively. We didn't have an instrument capable of real sustain, except what Jerry was doing.

137

1980 PHOTO USED AS THE BAND'S OFFICIAL SHOT

138

GARCIA: Having another percussion instrument in an all-percussion band was really too much of the same thing. The effect the piano had on the ensemble was something we could accomplish with guitars, so what we really needed was sustain.

WEIR: I guess desperation is the mother of invention. I figured you could get quite a bit of sustain with slide guitar, especially if you threw in a little bit of feedback and distortion. That's why I took up slide guitar.

It's a good thing your next keyboard player had a synthesizer and an organ.

GARCIA: That's what we wanted: somebody who would produce color. We were all *hungry* for color. Real hungry.

"Abraham and Isaac sittin' on a fence
You'd get right to work if you had any sense"

Why did it take the band so long to do something about these problems?

WEIR: We're procrastinators. The bigger the problem, the greater the procrastination.

LESH: Avoidance of confrontation is almost a religious point with us.

◆　　◆　　◆

The details are of no lasting importance. Sometime early in 1979 the decision was made to seek a replacement for Keith and Donna Godchaux. It was suggested that Brent Mydland of Bob Weir's band be given a shot at the job, since he played organ as well as piano and synthesizer and could also sing.

After leaving the Grateful Dead, Keith and Donna joined a Marin County band called Ghosts, which afforded greater opportunities for both of them to express themselves musically than they'd had with the Dead. But on July 21, 1980, Keith was critically injured in a car crash on a country road in Marin County. He died two days later without having regained consciousness.

ED PERLSTEIN

Donna has carried on with her musical pur-suits, and in 1982 she married a musician named David McKay.

◆　　◆　　◆

MYDLAND: Weir called me up one night to tell me there was a possibility the Dead might be looking for somebody else to play keyboards and asked if I was interested. I said, "Sure," and then I got a call a couple of weeks later saying they were definitely interested.

Bob told me some tunes they did, and I listened to *Shakedown Street*, which was their latest record. I learned some tunes I didn't need to—I think half the tunes I listened to we still don't do.

At the "audition" I was a little on edge, but I just figured either it's gonna work or it isn't. There's nothing you can do except play like you play; if it works, it works.

We only went through a few tunes, and a couple of those weren't even ones I'd listened to.

But I fell into them easily. They'd play through them once, and then we'd play them together. The idea was to see if I could play with the Grateful Dead the way they play.

HART: Brent was fighting it for a while. He didn't believe in the structureless form—he didn't think it was valid. I think he just came to this as a job. . . .

I wondered about Brent for a while. I was his toughest critic, in a way, because he didn't have the passion at first. Then his attitude changed. He relaxed, and his playing changed.

Until he saw the beauty in the music, I couldn't see the beauty in him. He knows now, and I really like him. I think his playing is really nice. He's a better player than when he started with the Grateful Dead, and he's doing more with what he has. But it was strange at first.

MYDLAND: They told me, "Don't worry about playing anything you've heard before from Keith or Pigpen; that's not what we want. Just play what you feel, be yourself, and think of dynamics." So on some songs I cop the theme of Keith's keyboards, but otherwise I just play my own stuff.

"Light the song with sense
and color
Hold away despair"

"The synthesizer was a bit of a problem at first. You have to have an idea of what you want and then find it on the instrument before you can use it," Brent explains. "Our music is so spur-of-the-moment that I might get an idea that makes me want to change a certain sound, but by the time I've figured out what I want, the music has changed again and it doesn't fit anymore. This is not the kind of group where you can work things out in advance."

Mydland now uses a Yamaha digital synthesizer with a wide range of extremely high-quality sounds that don't require furious knob-twisting in the middle of a song, so the Dead's hunger for color is at last being satisfied. When Mydland strikes up the harpsichord in "China Doll," it's the synthesizer you're hearing—that's how good its sound is.

11
Self-determination

ALL HE LOST HE SHALL REGAIN

"To me, the record companies have never been a malicious presence. . . .
They're more like a mindless juggernaut." —JERRY GARCIA

From the start, the Grateful Dead has been primarily a real-time experience, so making records has been less an effort to generate vinyl discs for sale to the public than another front on which to hassle with the real world and, more importantly, an arena in which to play out the various life-adventure scenarios of the writers, players, and technical wizards.

The Byzantine process of making *Aoxomoxoa* left the band deeply in debt to Warner Bros. The relatively inexpensive *Live Dead*, hustled into existence in hopes of quieting the corporate jackals, was an inadvertent masterpiece, but it hardly solved the band's financial problems.

Compared to its two studio predecessors, *Workingman's Dead* was done in the blink of an eye. The reasons were many and unavoidable: Their debt to Warner Bros. would grow with every hour of studio time, a financial situation that was bound to worsen as a result of the recent New Orleans bust, and things were weird on the management scene. . . . It just made sense to see if being careful could work for a change.

By coincidence—if you believe in such things as coincidences—Hunter, Garcia, and Lesh had recently completed a batch of handsome songs, and the band had played them into shape by the time the sessions got underway in February 1970. The lyricist's observations on the business of being a professional rock band made for a beautiful collection of images scattered around this group of songs, which shared a railroads-and-ragtime America atmosphere. Put a lunchbox in his hand and airbrush the shadow of a smoking chimney on the wall behind him and you have the portrait of the musician as wage-earner: *Workingman's Dead*. Of course, cover and title also served as an ironic reminder of an earlier Utopianism that was, for the moment, gone but not forgotten.

> "I gotta get down
> I gotta get down to the mine"

GARCIA: Most of the time when we're working on an album there's stuff going on in life that has more of our attention, and working on the album is like going to a job.

BARON WOLMAN

LESH CALLS THIS PICTURE OF KREUTZMANN "THE ROCKIN' K."

Workingman's Dead, which turned out to be our most significant album on a certain level, was the album we worked the least on [aside from the first record]. I think we spent nineteen or twenty days on it. Being busted in New Orleans was hanging over our heads, we were in the middle of a management hassle . . . all this other stuff was going on, and the record was almost beside the point compared to what we were going through.

♦   ♦   ♦

"When life looks like Easy
  Street
There is danger at your door"

Relations between the Dead and Warner Bros. were strained, to put it mildly, when the band proposed calling their 1971 live double LP *Skullfuck*. "*Skullfuck* was an *attitude*,"Lesh says by way of explanation.

142

BOB WEIR AT HOME, 1972

ANDY LEONARD

"They were difficult," one Warner Bros. executive recalls. "They didn't want any part of anything everyday—they wanted to be different.

"We at the company didn't feel that *Skullfuck* was an appropriate title for getting the album into, say, the department stores. Garcia said he would settle for fifteen thousand in sales if the album could go out with that title, but any decision that concerned the band had to involve everybody, and their *families* were involved in the decision as well.

"It was necessary to hold a meeting with all of them, but the record company's conference room wasn't big enough—the Dead had brought fifty-five people with them—so we had to rent the conference room at the Continental Hyatt House to discuss the *Skullfuck* question."

The album was released as *Grateful Dead* late in the summer of 1971. Ironically, it became the band's first gold record—largely due to a strong promotion campaign keying on live broadcasts of

GARCIA AT THE DEAD OFFICE AROUND THE TIME HIS FIRST SOLO ALBUM WAS RELEASED IN MARCH 1972

ROB SEIDEMANN

concerts in most of the cities the Dead played in the last three months of the year.

The first half of 1972 saw the release of solo albums by Garcia and Weir, each in its own way a masterpiece. While *Garcia* is a true solo effort—one musician's vision, executed mostly by himself with some help from his friends—*Ace* is in fact a Grateful Dead album consisting entirely of lead vocals and songs by Bob Weir.

Workingman's Dead and *American Beauty* were followed by Garcia's first solo album, *Garcia*, and *Ace*, which, although referred to as Bob Weir's album, is one of the best *Grateful Dead* albums of the lot. Some of the Dead's strongest and most enduring live material came from these two records—which is another one of the ironies surrounding the band. Maybe, just maybe, the Dead's committee/mob rule approach to life shouldn't be taken into the recording studio.

Weir was just coming into his own as a songwriter, and this project marked his transformation from Hunter's problem into Barlow's partner. It would also appear that since this was to be Weir's album rather than the band's, the players felt they should be more responsive to his wishes than they would otherwise have been. Six of the eight songs include the entire band (Dave Torbert played bass on "Greatest Story Ever Told"), and this time around they played the *songs*, not just their instruments. And as a bonus, the ensemble work on this version of "Playing in the Band" is about as close as they've ever come to achieving true Deadness in a recording studio.

Ace was the recording debut of the post-Pigpen edition of the Grateful Dead, featuring pianist Keith Godchaux and his vocalist wife, Donna, and demonstrating Weir's rapidly maturing songwriting skills.

◆　　◆　　◆

WEIR: I knew I was going to use Keith Godchaux on keyboards, because the Grateful Dead hadn't used him on record yet. When I told everybody else I had booked studio time for an album of my own, they said "Great—have fun."

After I had the songs put together and got into the studio, the other members of the Grateful

143

Dead started drifting in to volunteer their services. I kinda acted like Tom Sawyer whitewashing the fence—"*Welllll*, I wanna be careful and get just the right musicians for this record, y'know." And, of course, I ended up with the Grateful Dead on *Ace*, which I'd figured on up front.

♦ ♦ ♦

"Here's a half a dollar if
you dare
Double twist when you hit
the air"

The Dead decided to take their business away from the industry and try putting out their records their own way. "Our music is singular, and we saw no reason why our merchandising and marketing efforts shouldn't be singular as well," Weir explained in 1983. "The original idea was to create an alternative method of marketing music both on record and in concert. We figured if we put enough ingenuity into it we could come up with methods of marketing whereby the consumers would benefit as well as ourselves. We could make music more readily available and cheaper than it otherwise might be."

One of the Dead's major beefs with the industry was the quality of the pressing and packaging they could get. Believing that any reductions in the wholesale prices of Grateful Dead product would be kept by the middlemen rather than passed on to the consumers, they planned to

THE QUINTESSENTIAL QUINTET, 1971

BOB SEIDEMANN

spend more at the manufacturing end and, according to Weir, "put out a much finer product for the normal wholesale price. . . . better vinyl, more care in the recording, mastering, and pressing, et cetera. . . ."

Before the final decision was made and Grateful Dead Records was launched, some of the people involved met with Clive Davis, then head of Columbia Records. In his book, *Clive: Inside the Record Business* (William Morrow, 1975), Davis—who, ironically, landed the Dead for Arista Records in 1977—admitted that he was not pleased with the idea of a band running its own record company. "As a business executive, I found this a very threatening idea. . . . It could be a bad precedent for the industry if it worked."

Davis recalls telling them he thought they were "approaching some of the issues a little idealistically. . . . Only when they were convinced of the impracticality of alternative distribution arrangements did they discipline their imaginations and devote their attention to setting up a strong independent distributor network. . . ."

Joe Smith, who was the head of Warner Bros. when the Dead decided to strike out on their own, was a little more blunt: "They can't afford to have any disasters," he told the *Wall Street Journal*. "One bad record could wipe out their profit. This doesn't happen when artists record for the major record companies."

◆　　◆　　◆

GARCIA [1973]: It's dumb to complain about all that record company bullshit. If you're enough of an asshole to stick it up where they can shoot at it, you can't complain for getting shot. As far as I'm concerned, our whole record trip was our blunder, and we've been living with our mistake for all these years.

Now, hopefully, we're free to make our own mistakes.

"If mercy's in business
I wish it for you"

Pigpen's death early in 1973, the growing suspicion that they were again being guided by untrustworthy hands, and a tragically successful experiment in sound reinforcement all took their toll on the spiritual health of the community.

Bear and the rest of the sound wizards had proposed a system that gave each musician his own PA system. It worked, but it was expensive and huge. The Dead put it into operation anyway. It soon became obvious that hitting the road with two complete stages (leapfrogging each other so one could be setting up in the next town while the band played in this one) and this big PA—five semis worth of Grateful Dead hardware in all—in that gas-gouging summer of '74 was highly impractical.

◆　　◆　　◆

WEIR: We would go from hockey hall to hockey hall, selling them all out, and lose money every night. We couldn't make our payroll! We couldn't provide for the cost of carting this monster PA around.

There was also the fact that we couldn't fire anybody. And even if we *could* fire someone, we couldn't figure out who it was.

GARCIA: The decision to knock off in '74 began nearly a year earlier: "This isn't happening. We've got to hang it up." Economically, it wasn't working. . . .

"Believe it if you need it
Or leave it if you dare"

GARCIA: We were all pretty depressed. We felt it should be fun. It was out of our control, and nobody was really doing it because they liked it. We were doing it because we had to.

WEIR: There were a few people, and an attitude and a modus operandi, that we had to shake loose. We needed time off to see where we were stuck, and to see who would stick around.

GARCIA: Then we had to do a certain amount of work just to get into a position where we could quit.

Were you really prepared to live without the Grateful Dead?

WEIR: That was the greatest likelihood of all at that point, because everybody was getting involved in other stuff.

◆   ◆   ◆

"In and out of the garden he goes"

Mickey Hart, who had left the Dead in February 1971 for a variety of (mostly personal) reasons, came to Winterland on the last night of that "final" five-night stand in October of 1974, played in the band for the last two sets and eventually rejoined permanently.

Why did you leave the band in '71?

HART: There was something in my mind that I wanted to do. The road was getting to be a little too much for me, and there were also some minor squabbles, but mainly I wanted to find out what I sounded like—personally, not just in the Grateful Dead.

Dan Healy, Johnny D'Fonseca, and I built a studio at my house, and I went right to work on my album. [*Rolling Thunder*, released by Warner Bros. in 1972 and now out of print, included two Hart-Weir-Hunter collaborations which later entered the Dead's repertoire and appeared on *Ace*: "The Main Ten (Playing in the Band)" and "The Pump Song," which evolved into "Greatest Story Ever Told." In addition to Hunter and Weir, Garcia and Lesh contributed to the record, along with a host of San Francisco musicians and David Crosby and Stephen Stills.]

The Grateful Dead seems like the only place where you can walk out and walk back in without saying anything. No answers or excuses—one day I left, and three and a half years later I showed up and played again.

THE "WALL OF SOUND," MARCH 1974. FIVE HUGE TRAILERS FULL OF SPEAKERS, AMPLIFIERS, STAGES, SCAFFOLDING, LIGHTS, AND INSTRUMENTS COST THE DEAD HUGE SUMS OF MONEY.

MARY ANN MAYER

. . . Either you *are* Grateful Dead or you aren't, so when I came back I was just back. There was no asking. I finished what I had to do, and I was ready to play. I knew they wouldn't forget me. I knew that when the time was right it would come together again.

WEIR: Mickey came down to Winterland figuring, "This is the last night—I'd better get my drums down there." He didn't want to miss out. He showed up at the back door with his drums, and we said, "Set 'em up!"

HART: I couldn't see it going down without me. It just wouldn't be right. So I brought my drums down and played during the second set, and it was pretty good—good enough to be reborn, in a way. I got off really heavy; everybody in the band got off really heavy. The monster came out that night. . . . It was totally spontaneous, and that's when Grateful Dead music has always been at its best. When we work something out, it could be any other bozo.

♦ ♦ ♦

GARCIA: Filming five nights [the "final" run at Winterland in October of 1974] was a gamble. The possibility was that we would ideally have a good night in the five, so let's go for broke. But the only way we'd get it was if everybody shot *all* the time. . . . I ended up with about 150 hours of film.

The movie's energy is a good *movie* example of the Grateful Dead experience. . . . The first part, after the animation, has a roughness—it's a little fuzzy, a little hot, and not really gathered. Then, later on, the whole thing composes itself and becomes clear. The cinematography in the second half is really incredible.

That's a way of expressing this thing: When

147

GARCIA PICKIN' AND GRINNIN' WITH STEVE MARTIN (*CENTER*) AND THE NITTY GRITTY DIRT BAND'S JOHN McEUEN AT A BLUEGRASS FESTIVAL IN MARIN COUNTY, CALIFORNIA, APRIL 1974

JON SIEVERT

GOLDEN GATE PARK, SAN FRANCISCO, AUGUST 1975, ONE OF ONLY FOUR PUBLIC APPEARANCES BY THE DEAD DURING THAT YEAR

JIM MARSHALL

you go out there and play, things are confusing at first. It's noisy, you're still trying to tune up, and the whole first half is like settling into something. . . . The film uses that kind of energy to pick up on the restlessness of the whole thing.

Why is there no relation between Steal Your Face *and the movie, both of which document the same event?*

GARCIA: Phil wanted to go through the tapes and pick out what *he* liked, for his own reasons. . . . If anyone wants to have some concept of what Phil likes, that's a good album. The movie was my project, for the most part.

LESH: I said to the band, "For this album I volunteer me and Bear. . . . I'd like to put out on this live album *only* tunes that we've never put out on a live album before," and I said that about three times to make sure everybody agreed. If *Steal Your Face* is what I "like," it's because I like the Grateful Dead with zits. We don't do anything without zits on it.

HUNTER: I thought the same thing about *Steal Your Face* as my most unfavorite critic, the man I loved to hate: Lester Bangs of *Creem.* He said, very succinctly, "*Steal Your Face,* HAH! *Steal Your Money* is more like it!"

◆　　◆　　◆

GARCIA: We went into the studio [in January 1975] with *no* preconceptions and *no* material. We were recording at Weir's house, and it was a chance to hang out together and to let ideas evolve from absolutely nothing—a completely untested situation all the way through. We weren't putting the material together and then having everybody learn the tunes and then going out and performing—'cause we *weren't performing!* We were going to spend six months just mulling over stuff.

WEIR: Mickey came by with a Japanese rooster one night while we were working on *Blues for Allah.* Next thing we knew he was involved in the recording, and the next thing he was back in the band.

"The sullen wings of fortune
beat like rain
You're back in Terrapin for
good or ill again."

Was it like he'd never left?

WEIR: No, it wasn't like that at all.

HART: Throughout "Blues for Allah" there are crickets on the basic track. I got them from a cricket connection, of course. We kept them alive, fifty of them, and we miked the box. We recorded them, then we slowed 'em down, sped 'em up, played them backwards at half speed. . . . They sounded like whales, and they sounded like chirping birds.

We made this tape called "The Desert." Garcia was engineering, and I was in the studio playing all my little percussion things—bells, metal, glass. We had to be really quiet, because I was playing some of this metal and wood stuff with a paintbrush!

We made about a twenty-minute track that changed from wood to glass to crickets . . . mostly my percussion instruments. Then Garcia gated it with a vocoder, saying "Allah . . . Al—lah" into the microphone. You don't hear his voice—what you hear is the whole desert saying "Allah." That's why there's a track called "Unusual Occurrences in the Desert."

After we finished, we liberated the crickets on Weir's mountain. And for years after, Bobby had exotic crickets living outside his house. . . .

GARCIA: I like *Blues for Allah* as an experiment; in terms of the life experience of making the record, it was really a boon.

149

◆

12 Recording, Part 2

KEEP ON ROLLING, JUST A MILE TO GO

"We can't manufacture intensity in the studio. We can't say, 'Now we're going to be sensitive,' and 'Now we're going to be soulful.' It has to really be happening, or it's not happening at all." —JERRY GARCIA

"William Tell has stretched
    his bow
'Til it won't stretch no
    further . . ."

The self-determination movie played itself out, and by the time *Blues for Allah* was ready for release, the Dead operation was in need of financial relief. The good ol' Grateful Dead tradition of giving people enough rope to hang them all left Grateful Dead Records and Round Records in a bind of major proportions.

A deal was struck with United Artists Records which held together long enough to get *Blues for Allah* (September 1975) and *Steal Your Face* (June 1976) released, and the members of the Grateful Dead put away their briefcases and went back to being musicians first and foremost.

Following the dissolution of their own record company, the Dead signed with Arista Records, whose president, Clive Davis, presumably refrained from crowing over the failure of the Dead's ambitious scheme to deliver themselves

and their fans from the music industry and people like him.

"Gone are the broken eyes we
    saw through in dreams
Gone, both dream and lie"

WEIR: With the reintroduction of Mickey, the band reached critical mass as to the number of ideas and opinions expressed—most vocally expressed—at any given time. We just had too many horses pulling in too many directions, and we were faced with the prospect of taking *years* to make a record. Or we could try a producer, which we hadn't done in twelve years or so . . .

GARCIA: When we signed with Arista, we went with a spirit of cooperation, thinking, We've tried things our way—we've had our own record company, we've produced ourselves—it'd be interesting to try somebody else's approach and see where that takes us.

WEIR: A producer is a guy who spends the bulk of his time in the studio. I spend most of my time on stage, and I've developed a lot of technique for my onstage presentation. He's developed a whole lot of technique for working in the studio, so he's going to be more in touch with what's going on in there. It's an immensely complex instrument, and he plays it.

GARCIA: Our records have always been neither here nor there. We wanted some fresh ears, and that's part of the reason the idea of a producer didn't seem outrageous to us. We're very conscious of how easy it is to get into your own trip so much that you have no objectivity at all.

"I asked him for mercy
He gave me a gun"

WEIR: We've got a number of different writers, and even if we're working with a producer, everybody is at least coproducing his own tunes. You don't stand much of a chance of getting real consistency under those circumstances, so you don't even shoot for it.

KEITH OLSEN: I remembered how they'd sounded when I'd heard them play live several years ago. They blew me away, and I'd always wondered why they couldn't get that on record.

I told them *Blues for Allah* sounded like they'd rushed through it, and then I found out they'd spent five months making it. "Five months?" I said. "Really?"

Garcia said, "Well, let me rephrase that. We spent four and a half months trying to figure out what we should do first, and the last two weeks recording."

WEIR: Our past albums were like Dagwood sandwiches: You had to listen to them thirty or forty times to hear everything we dubbed in. We all have very strong opinions about what should be done with a song, and it gets too cumbersome in the studio. If you made a suggestion to put something in, then you'd have to let everybody else put in their suggestions, too. We needed one authority to make the decisions.

Also, Keith Olsen is very short, so no one would hit him.

HART: Keith Olsen is a good producer and a good engineer. He was qualified, but he had a problem: He didn't know the Grateful Dead. He tried to mold the Grateful Dead in his own image.

OLSEN: There were some trying moments, grinding away trying to figure out if what we were doing was right. It's a fine line. I didn't want to dictate to the Dead, because I would have destroyed a rapport, but I didn't want to let them dictate to me. I wanted every performance to come out of them, but I wanted them to be open to ideas like a Tom Scott solo on "Estimated Prophet."

AT THE END OF THE DEAD'S SUMMER 1976 "COMEBACK" TOUR, SIX BATHING BEAUTIES AND A TUXEDOED BILL GRAHAM ("MR. DONNA") CAME ONSTAGE WITH FLOWERS FOR THE BAND.

JON SIEVERT

WORKING ON *TERRAPIN STATION* AT SOUND CITY IN VAN NUYS, CALIFORNIA, WITH PRODUCER KEITH OLSEN AT THE CONTROLS

PETER SIMON

HART: He did one of the most disrespectful things that has ever happened to me. "Terrapin Flyer," on the second side of *Terrapin,* was supposed to be a timbale solo and a duet between me and Garcia. Olsen erased one of my beautiful timbale tracks in Europe and replaced it with all these strings. When he played it for me, my mouth *dropped . . .*

WEIR: One of the reasons we don't make good records, generally, is that we don't know the material when we're recording it. We sometimes don't really know a song until *years* after recording it.

I wasn't altogether pleased with how "Sugar Magnolia" came out when we recorded it in the studio. It wasn't everything it should have been. I didn't know how to tell anybody that, but as soon as we took it out on the road it immediately evolved into a whole lot more than what we'd

just put on vinyl. At that point it became exactly what I'd envisioned.

When you present a song from the stage, that's where it comes together. "Estimated Prophet" is *the* most graphic example of that theory. We learned the song in the studio, basically, while we were trying to put it on tape. We played one weekend in southern California—played the song at two gigs—then went back into the studio and got it in three takes. It was cohesive where it had been a disheveled mess. Presenting it to people as a piece makes a world of difference.

On the other hand, we did "Samson and Delilah" for a couple of tours before recording it and still didn't get it on record the way we should have. That song fairly crackled and growled in concert, and on record it was kinda tame. I don't know. . . .

Even so, we should make a blanket policy of

PETER SIMON

154

not recording anything we haven't played on stage.

MYDLAND: Bob and Jerry are kinda like polar opposites. Jerry's melodies and chord progressions are easy to get into—comfortable. Bob will go to the other extreme, with off-the-wall stuff that doesn't seem like it goes together. But after hearing it for a while, it starts to sound right.

When Jerry's got a new tune, he comes in and just starts playing it—from the top to the end. Then he goes back to the top and plays it to the end. He just plays, and you fit in. If you blow it, you just keep following along. If you don't get it this time you'll get it next time. He doesn't say, "Bridge coming up!"—it just happens, and, "Oh, that's where the bridge is! Well, I'll get it next time."

Bob doesn't usually have a melody. He's usually got the lyrics and some kind of idea of what he wants to happen first. He's got a chorus . . . The melody will change—until it's put down on the record, I think. The whole contour of the tune is different every time we play it. So you have to keep learning his song until it's on vinyl.

We learned most of the tunes for *Go to Heaven* while we were recording them. With Bob there's no other way, because he's *writing* them as we record them [*laughs*]. You don't know quite what

direction the words are going to go in, so you don't know what kind of mood to be playing in— "Is this a song about a killer or a lover?"

You've worked with three different producers on three albums. Certainly Keith Olsen [Terrapin Station], *Lowell George* [Shakedown Street], *and Gary Lyons* [Go to Heaven] *have different styles; what have you gotten out of those experiences?*

GARCIA: For me, it was interesting to see how other people deal with the Grateful Dead. I think that part of it alone was worthwhile, even if there was nothing else to it but the way they went about working with us.

A producer has to make an effort to understand what you're doing musically . . . we were lucky in that each of those guys paid some dues to understand where Grateful Dead music is at and what we were trying to accomplish with the material we were working with. They spent time with us while we were rehearsing and asked musical questions that made some sense.

They all had their different ways of dealing with that level of understanding. There were lots of little production licks that I picked up from each of those guys and added to my vocabulary of useful little things. There's always something to learn from working with other people.

WEIR, GARCIA, AND PRODUCER GARY LYONS (GO TO HEAVEN) SIGN AUTOGRAPHS AT A FUND-RAISING RECEPTION FOLLOWING A BENEFIT CONCERT AT THE OAKLAND COLISEUM, JANUARY 13, 1980.

13
Deadheads

ALL OF MY FRIENDS COME TO SEE ME LAST NIGHT

"It seems as though there's a certain kind of person in every generation . . . who can dig what we're doing. We're not trying to win converts or anything; it's there to be discovered." —JERRY GARCIA

"Believe it if you need it
If you don't, just pass it on"

Turning people on to the Grateful Dead is not an easy thing to do. The Dead are an acquired taste, and not very easy to acquire at that.

The records sure aren't the way—everybody knows Dead albums aren't a patch on their live action. Tapes of concerts are a better idea, and they're available for the cost of a blank cassette from your friendly neighborhood Deadhead, but tapes can't transduce the *je ne sais quoi* that fills the hall with electricity at a good gig. No, the way to initiate someone is to haul him bodily to a Dead concert—or two or three, in order to ensure that the inculcation takes.

Imagine the first baseball game you ever attended. You had no idea what was going on, but once in a while something took place that caused people to stand up and shout. Between those brief periods of exciting activity were long spells of organized but unfathomable activity that looked like fun and definitely made sense to the people around you.

Baseball is not a game for impatient spectators; it takes several trips to the ballpark for a neophyte to start picking up on the subtleties and continuity of the game. But once you're hooked, there are a number of different levels on which to appreciate it. Each game can be taken on its own merits as a contest or an exhibition of athletic skills; there's the pennant race, that do-or-die game on which rest the team's World Series hopes; individual players matter to some fans more than the teams and standings; and there are people who just plain love the logic of the game regardless of the teams or the outcome (which must explain Chicago Cubs fans).

And so it is with the Grateful Dead. "They don't need to decorate a room or use strobe lights or wear tight pants," says Bill Graham. "They don't look right, they're not sexy, and they don't have a stage show, but they can just *absorb* you—which is something very few groups, even on their best nights, can do."

It's as though they were just hanging out together and playing music. They don't introduce songs, they don't use flash pots or backup singers,

◆

they don't have a front man in a leather union suit and studded dog collar huffing and puffing sincerely between songs about how "it sure is good to be back in [local reference] again!"

There's more to it than music, obviously, but everything about this phenomenon stems from the music and eventually comes back to it. Never mind the records and the videos and the commercial tie-ins, man—the Grateful Dead just play their music.

♦ ♦ ♦

BILL GRAHAM: It's not just the music that gets me off. The greatest pleasure I get is from seeing and feeling the effect of Dead's music on whoever's there. Not only are all guards dropped, but it's as if the *tsouris* door closes and the fresh air door opens. It's "time out, world—I'm here to have a good time."

When the Dead walk out onto the stage at the beginning of the show and tune up for a good five minutes, you'll hear people who have never met these musicians talking about them the way they'd talk about neighbors or cousins. It's a warm, ongoing relationship, a gathering of relatives who don't know each other.

KREUTZMANN: I never have understood what's popular and what isn't, but I know there's a big difference between our audience and other bands' audiences. We do have a unique audience. It's the part of society that doesn't want to be ruled that comes to hear us—and that's kinda cool.

GRAHAM: So many Dead fans say, "God, I need a dose. I've just got to have a hit of the Dead." Then they fly to Denver. These people want to think and feel along with those words again.

Whatever is going on in the world, when you get into their building, it's "time out." That is the largest non-organized club in this planet. And where it meets, nobody gets hurt.

EILEEN LAW: I get letters from parents saying we're the only concert they'll allow their kids to go to. You don't see fights going on . . .

"No one is forsaken
No one is a liar"

THE GRATEFUL DEAD AND SOME OF THE FIRST DEADHEADS, 1967

TOM COPI

BARLOW: I'm glad I'm part of something that provides people with a sense of community and the feeling that they aren't alone in trying to preserve these virtues and these ways of looking at humankind.

The community aspect is of major importance. Everybody says hello, does little patois things with each other. . . . They're a lot happier with the floating community of Deadheads than the average American is with the society he has with his fellow man.

Most people nowadays don't come from any place. They live in suburban areas where you live in your house and the next guy lives in his house, and they don't have the kind of relationships where you don't have to *ask* somebody for help. In a community, it doesn't make any difference what troubles you've got with your neighbors—if they really get their ass in a sling, you help out.

Communities used to be founded on geographic or economic bases. This one is based on something vaguely spiritual, and it has no geographic location—but it is just as much a community as any mining town.

> "Some come to laugh the past
> away
> Some come to make it just
> one more day"

A Grateful Dead audience today is like one of those high-tech video freeze-frames of sports events, where the image stops but the runner keeps going. The band members have moved on and grown both musically and personally (although their situation may allow them to remain forever young), but the media's image of the band and the behavior of a large segment of their audience remain frozen in the tie-dyed, Indian-blanketed glory days of the Summer of Love.

The "hippie" era ended and the Haight-Ashbury scene dried up because the numbers, not the ideas, were wrong. The concept of a community where people cared for each other but didn't interfere in each other's lives was a good one, but it drew too many parasites and promoters and collapsed under the weight of its own idealism.

"I hope you all have been paying pretty close attention out there, on account of we're going to be passing out a quiz any minute now. Those of you who have been hollering requests for songs we've already done tonight, I know you're not going to do very well."
—BOB WEIR

The Grateful Dead came by their system of self-government by non-government honestly, when the Haight-Ashbury was a neighborhood and not yet a magnet for runaways and dropouts. By the time the big dream went bust and left most of the dreamers to fend for themselves, the Dead's own community was strong enough in terms of the commitment of its members and its economic viability in the real world to go on operating more or less on its own terms.

The Dead were also so closely identified with the acid-soaked mind-music of San Francisco that, intentionally or otherwise, they became the keepers of the multi-colored flame.

> "In another time's forgotten
> space
> Your eyes looked from your
> mother's face"

159

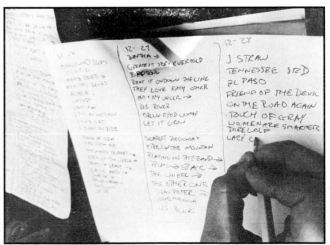

PETER SIMON

Hippies are as rare as clean air and condors in the Hell-in-a-bucket, survivalist environs of post-Me Generation America, but impressive concentrations of people who live That Way and dress Like That can be seen wherever the Grateful Dead perform.

And their numbers are growing. "There are more hippies now than there were in 1967," observes John Barlow. "They're the same age as we were, and they look just like we did." Thousands who were unborn or in diapers when the Dead lived together at 710 Ashbury in San Francisco are now learning tribal arts and laws of diet and hygiene which have been lovingly preserved and handed down for two decades.

It may be a little harder to pull off in the eighties, but dropping out is still (or again) an attractive alternative to middle-class life for some people. The values shared by the hippie-types offer freedom from material ambition and social restrictions, all in the name of harmless good fun.

For some, Deadheaddom is a permanent refuge. Rather than put forth the effort to compete for goods and status in the straight world, they escape into this community, which accepts all comers as they are, expecting nothing in particular from them, demanding little of them, and posting no minimum rules of social conduct.

This highly visible segment of the Grateful Dead crowd is an odd and anachronistic lot. Its members sport unfashionably optimistic and/or fatalistic world views, furnish their lives in Low-Rent rather than High-Tech (except, of course, for their stereos), and work at jobs rather than professions or careers so they can unplug from employment and/or residence any time they want to hit the road with the Dead.

"Beneath the sweet, calm face of the sea . . ."

These retrograde dropout types are only the most visible of the Deadheads. This community splashes across all the usual demographic barriers rock bands face, attracting middle-aged professionals and hard-working young Americans as well as students and hippies. Some of the casually dressed folks at Dead concerts will prove to be pretty well-groomed on close inspection. They just don't wear their work clothes to the concert.

Plenty of Deadheads fly their freak flags on the inside and have interests beyond their camping plans for New Year's and the pot they got for the shows and the relative merits of various microphones. There are Deadheads who follow the Grand Prix and go to the opera. Hell, there's even a *member* of the Dead who follows the Grand Prix and goes to the opera.

"Yes, believe it or not, I was a Deadhead." —STEVE PARISH

Some Deadheads hold responsible positions in law, medicine, computer science, education, and other highly skilled fields. There are Deadheads who play tennis, live in fine homes, don't take drugs, and know what capital gains are—and even have some. There are Deadheads who drive BMWs, frequent trendy restaurants and understand their wine lists, and who wear alligator shirts. Hell, there's even a *member* of the Dead who wears alligator shirts.

Not all Deadheads' diplomas were get-out-of-town presents from the local authorities. Some of these people dropped out in their minds but toed the line long enough to finish school, then chose the Dead life over the fast track. They hold their degrees in the same kind of esteem Bob Weir does his gold records (one hangs in the bathroom).

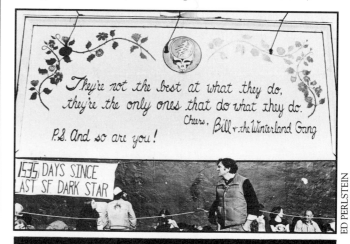

They're not the best at what they do, they're the only ones that do what they do. Cheers, Bill + the Winterland Gang

P.S. And so are you!

1535 DAYS SINCE LAST SF DARK STAR

ED PERLSTEIN

THE CLOSING OF WINTERLAND, DECEMBER 31, 1978. AS THE CONCERT ENDED, BILL GRAHAM ASKED THE FANS NOT TO REMOVE THE SEATS OR TAKE ANY OTHER "SOUVENIRS," SINCE THE BUILDING WAS NOT HIS TO DISMANTLE.

Some of these Deadheads are entrepreneurs who earn their living in the Deadheads' counter-economy of herbs, jewelry, clothing, art, and devotional aids. Some are actors, journalists, artists, carpenters—independent businesspeople who pursue their own goals and look to the Dead for inspiration and an escape valve, a bright spot on the calendar. These people can travel freely between the two worlds and function more or less normally most of the time. Hell, there's even a *member* of the Dead who functions more or less normally most of the time.

> "I just wonder if you shouldn't
>   feel
> Less concern about the deep
>   unreal . . ."

WEIR: We, and particularly Garcia, are the cloak and scepter of a spiritual cult that we and he never wanted. We are a musical aggregation first and foremost, but people advance spiritual qualities to us which may or may not be important.

Everyone has to have some sort of cosmology, or life won't be rewarding. The only difference is that ours leaks into the media.

KREUTZMANN: Sometimes we tell a joke and it's taken as gospel by the Deadheads. We gotta wink a little harder.

A guy I know who does boat tours on the Colorado River swears Phil Lesh once came to him in the shape of a train, hooting by in the night to tell him, "Fear not—'Truckin' ' will be heard in these parts again soon."

HUNTER: That Phil—you never know what he'll be up to next.

You don't reject that idea out of hand——

HUNTER: I reject very little out of hand about this scene—and I don't accept very much in hand except what I personally experience.

> "You and me bound to spend
>   some time
> Wond'rin' what to choose . . ."

TOM DAVIS [comedian and Deadhead]: Everybody who's ever altered his consciousness and gone to a Grateful Dead concert has had the feeling that he affects the band. I myself have

162

SOUNDMAN DAN HEALY (*RIGHT*) AND THE TAPERS, WHO HAD A SECTION OF SEATS TO THEMSELVES AT BERKELEY IN OCTOBER 1984

DAVID GANS

blurted that out to band members once or twice, and they've sort of . . . "Yeah, we felt it . . . *Sure*."

GARCIA: People have reported that experience to us so many times—"You looked at me and I knew what you were going to play"; "I knew what you were going to play before you played it"; and all those variations. I can't pretend that it doesn't happen, and I can't discount it. I have to admit there's some validity to it, even though I'm distrustful of anything that's invisible or occult and can't be measured, tasted, or touched.

HART: Do you know what a psychopomp is? It's an escort of souls into the other world. The Grateful Dead play music, but that's not *all* we're doing. We're doing something else besides entertaining. We have the ability to transform. People come to be changed, and we change 'em.

Why is it that you can bring some people to it but you can't make them get it?

HART: Some people aren't ready to change. They don't come into the environment with a sense of openness. If you come to it with a lot of prejudices, you'll walk away with twice as many. But if you come to it wanting to have fun and be

moved, it'll make you look inside and think of things you never thought of before. It makes other realities seem common . . . but I don't want to get into cosmic mumbo-jumbo.

All the Grateful Dead demands is that you have a positive attitude. And by the way, you don't have to take acid or any other drug to appreciate what the Grateful Dead does. Acid alters the experience in certain respects; each drug alters it in a different way.

"Never could reach it
Just slips away when I try . . ."

GARCIA: . . . We're in the same position as the Deadheads about that phenomenon, really—the magic side of it. Everybody experiences it on their own terms, but for me as a player it's this thing that you can't make happen—but when it's happening, you can't stop it. I've tried to analyze it on every level I can gather together, and all the intellectual exercise in the world doesn't do a fucking thing to explain it to any degree of satisfaction.

The Grateful Dead has some kind of intuitive

163

WINTERLAND BEFORE THE DOORS OPEN, NEW YEAR'S EVE, 1978

RICHARD McCAFFREY

thing. I don't know how it works, but I recognize it phenomenologically. It's been reported to me hugely from the audience, and we've compared notes among ourselves in the band. But all we can really do is agree that we'll keep doing this thing—whatever it is—and that our best attitude toward it is a sort of stewardship, in which we are the custodians of this thing.

So the Grateful Dead may be immortal, but these men who play in the band are not.

GARCIA: That's exactly the way we feel. It takes the responsibility out of our hands, and that's a comfortable feeling. It's scary if you feel like you're responsible for it; that's a lot of energy to be responsible for.

> "Them voices tellin' me
> They say you'll soon receive me"

GARCIA: Sometimes they get a little excited, but you have to have a little bit of empathy, because the Grateful Dead can be very powerful and people can get sucked into it in a way that can be very harmful to them.

164

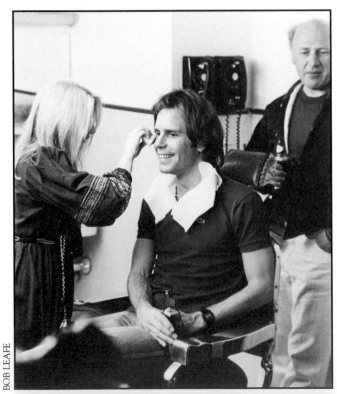

BOB LEAFE

THERE'S EVEN A *MEMBER* OF THE DEAD WHO WEARS ALLIGATOR SHIRTS. (THAT'S KEN KESEY STANDING BEHIND WEIR.)

There's a certain human weirdness that happens because of the high-energy nature of the thing. It's that moth-to-the-flame syndrome: Certain people become fixated on the Grateful Dead.

> "My time comin' any day . . ."

GARCIA: Once in a while some soul out there overamps, and all of a sudden there's a guy banging on the door with a whole weird Grateful Dead universe woven up with images from our stuff.

HARRY POPICK: Once when we were in Florida around Thanksgiving, most of the band and crew went out to dinner at a restaurant on the [Intracoastal] Waterway. We were sitting in the open-air part, by the water, and we noticed a kid hanging out kind of close. He was young, not dressed very well, and he was just sort of *right there*, watching. He was looming, and we felt uncomfortable.

Parish went over to the guy and asked him if he'd mind backing off a little bit. He walked away, and Steve came back to the table.

After a while the guy came back. Phil Giuliano, one of our catering people, saw him and said to me, "That guy's on top of us again. I'm going to go talk to him."

As [Giuliano] walked toward him, the guy pulled out what looked like a gun.

LESH: It turned out to be the kind of gun that's used to drive nails into concrete. It fires real blanks.

POPICK: Very quickly, everyone at the table—about twenty people—realized what was going on. A lot of people stood up. . . . In a matter of seconds, Steve Parish was walking straight at the guy, eyeball to eyeball, with this gun leveled right at him. Steve kept walking, grabbed the gun by the muzzle, and pushed it down—and prevented whatever might have happened.

LESH: He was saying, "I want to see Garcia. Where's Jerry?" Well, Jerry wasn't there . . .

WEIR: I didn't see the gun until it was on the ground. I picked it up and threw it in the canal . . . and then the guy was thrown into the canal. He wasn't beaten up or anything, he was just belayed and, uh, bathed.

POPICK: One of our other catering people is a lifeguard, and he jumped in and pulled the guy out. And then he walked away. We didn't call the police or anything. . . .

WEIR: The guy just had a head full of snakes . . .

"When it's done and over
A man is just a man"

Attempts by heroes to demystify themselves usually serve only to deepen the mystique, as Robert Hunter illustrated in a fable titled "Dilbert and the Plumber," which appeared in the Dead's 1983–84 concert program.

The good Dilbert was fascinated to discover that water always swirls down drains counterclockwise. The fact itself didn't impress him as much as the realization that this phenomenon is "consistent at the same time as being utterly arbitrary."

Some time later, the Dilbert found himself in the Southern hemisphere, where water swirls *clockwise* down the drain. This observation proved that his "arbitrary but consistent fact had only a relative validity—and relative validity you can find everywhere, even within reason itself." Not of itself a shattering insight into the ways of reality, perhaps, but it was on the Dilbert's mind when he was shipwrecked, washed ashore, and discovered, wandering in a daze, by a tribe of Bozos.

Over and over he murmured, "On the left hand it goes North and on the right hand South." When he regained his senses he found the Bozos repeating the phrase and "looking rather blissful."

Then the Dilbert said, "In between it may go straight down," upon which he was invited to become their king. He refused, so the Bozos elected him Saint and pressed him for teachings.

He explained the prosaic origin of his mumbled message, but the Bozos took this as "an elaborately cloaked metaphor," and their beliefs remained unshakable.

Which goes to show that you can always tell a Deadhead, but you can't tell him much.

◆　◆　◆

WEIR: When the Grateful Dead True Religion incorporates, I get to be in charge of making the mitres and stuff like that. We'll get some great hats. You may refer to me as "your holiness" from now on . . .

Maybe the band'll get together every three hundred years or so and reincarnate or make a reappearance. We'll work something out; you'll be among the first to know.

"What shall we say,
Shall we call it by a name?"

LESH: We used to say that every place we played was church. It was a pretty far-out church, but that was how we felt.

This is a pretty tolerant religion, isn't it?

GARCIA: Well, uh, (*harumph*) . . . That word has a lot of . . . *negative* to it. . . . I don't think a religion is what this is.

We're not saying what it is; we're not creating dogma. There's no central thing which is absolutely true that everybody can know about it.

LESH: We respect other people's experience of it just like we respect our own. It's like the sun, and we're all orbiting around it. By the very nature of that situation, we each look at it in a different way.

GARCIA: Right, but its warmth falls on *all* of us.

But it does fulfill the role of religion for a lot of Deadheads. Many belong to this to the exclusion of——

GARCIA: That's okay, too, because on a certain level it's a religion to me, too. But I don't like the word *religion*. It's a bad word.

Well, let's assign a new word to it.

GARCIA: I don't want to assign any word to it. Why limit it? I want it to continue to surprise me.

An experiment?

GARCIA: I experiment with my little part of it as much as I can. That's one of the reasons I know it isn't us. This is not something that we're cooking up . . .

LESH: Who could have cooked up something like this? None of us, in our wildest dreams.

GARCIA: Right, and you can't manipulate it or control it like you can a religion. That's one of the reasons why you can trust it. It's out there; it ain't in here.

165

LESH: We're just a piece of it.

GARCIA: That's right. We're not *it*——

LESH: No. *It* is informing all of us.

GARCIA: So our opinions are just that: *our* opinions. Whatever terms anyone experiences it on are the right terms.

But the Grateful Dead is something people attach their spiritual beings to——

LESH: An object of faith, perhaps.

It's like that for me. Even when I'm not satisfied—"This is getting lame, and I don't want to come back again"—I come back.

LESH: Because you know we'll try again.

GARCIA: We're sticking with it for that same reason. And to me, that's too large an idea for a word.

"St. Stephen with a rose"

BARLOW: This *beautiful* woman came up to me and said, "Are you the road manager?" I said yes, and she said, "I'll be right back," and she went away.

She came back with about a bushel of the most beautiful long-stemmed roses I'd ever seen. They weren't greenhouse roses, they'd been grown in the wild. They were amazing.

She said, "Dispose of them as you see fit."

I had practically everybody on the stage holding roses—often awkwardly and with some puzzlement, but holding roses. I even had Steve Parish holding a rose.

I started to give one to Garcia, and he gave me a really black look. I said, "Come on, man, it's the Sufi symbol of truth."

He said, "Do you know how many roses have been *thrown* at me?"

"Well, let me try to hand you one." He took it, and he walked quite a ways with it, and then he laid it gently down on something and walked off.

Immediately thereafter, I understood. I still had lots of roses, and I figured that since everybody was in such a marvelous mood out in the audience, the thing to do was to throw them the rest of the roses. And I saw people fight *mercilessly* for the Sufi symbol of truth.

"Gotta get down to the Cumberland mine
That's where I mainly spend my time"

BARLOW: When the band played at Radio City Music Hall [October 1980], Weir and Garcia were interviewed live on "Good Morning America." ABC had some taped interviews with Deadheads waiting in line for tickets, and one kid of about twenty said, "The Dead—that's where most of my money goes. I just love 'em so much."

So the straight lady asks Garcia what he thinks about that, and he answered, "What the hell do you think *we* do?"

POPICK: You know how people are always standing by the road on the way to gigs holding up signs that say I NEED A TICKET and I NEED A MIRACLE? One time, driving to the Greek Theatre in Berkeley, I saw one guy with his hands in that position, holding up an *imaginary* sign!

◆　　◆　　◆

The Grateful Dead's music has always appealed to a broad spectrum of fan types, as a look around at any of their concerts will show. Someone who dances through the whole show might not care a fig about lyrics; fans of the Dead's songcraft may be less concerned with the technical quality of the instrumentals than with the energy of the vocals; some people invariably hit the snack bar when certain slow tunes come up; devotees of the guitar players may grow impatient with the drum solos, and so on. A woman once asked me to make her a tape of a particular concert and said, "Just put the song parts in, okay? I don't care about the jazzy stuff in between."

As the years have gone by and the myth of the Grateful Dead has deepened, a growing proportion of the audience seems to be coming more for the social context of a Dead show than its musical content. To a band that wants the music to be genuine and unique every time, an audience that offers its support unequivocally can be a decidedly mixed blessing. It's understood that sometimes the music has to get painful before it can get pretty, but the Dead sometimes find themselves applauded for golden moments and loud mistakes with equal enthusiasm. Imagine drawing your

166

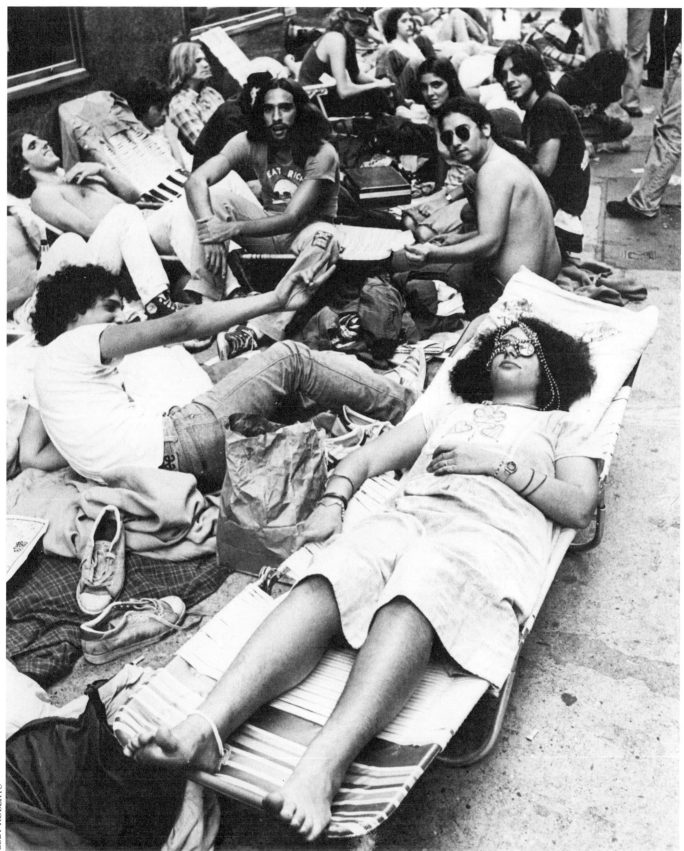

WAITING FOR TICKETS AT RADIO CITY MUSIC HALL, NEW YORK CITY, 1980

livelihood from an audience that allows you to pursue your art freely but often overlooks the best of the results!

♦   ♦   ♦

WEIR: The undiscriminating and unconditional adulation and love of those people doesn't do a whole lot for the music, I'll say. When the crowd goes wild after we've rendered a dismal set, I don't think they should clap at all. They should run us out of town on a rail—but they never do.

I don't think our audience is very critical, but they do know that we are pretty much the only meaningful alternative in popular music. The rest of it all sounds pretty similar, and we're not like the rest of it.

"You needn't gild the lily,
Offer jewels to the sunset . . .
Everything promised is delivered
to you"

BARLOW: I like the Deadheads. I don't understand them very well—they're a constant source of mystery . . .

And they're as harmless as can be.

BARLOW: In my part of the world, that's not generally thought of as a compliment. But the older I get and the more I see of the human race, the more I think that "He is harmless" is a good thing to say of someone.

♦   ♦   ♦

WEIR [January 8, 1978]: It's also Uncle Bill Graham's birthday. And it kinda caught us by surprise, so we didn't have time to go out and buy anything special or elaborate for him.

The best we could do on short notice was to give him a new name. So now, instead of Uncle Bill Graham, it's Uncle Bobo Graham. [*The band plays "Happy Birthday to You" to wild applause.*] So happy birthday, Uncle Bobo.

LESH: Say, "Happy birthday, Uncle Bobo!" [*The audience complies, with gusto.*]

AN ACOUSTIC SET AT RADIO CITY MUSIC HALL, NEW YORK CITY, OCTOBER 1980. BRENT MYDLAND IS NOT SHOWN

GRAHAM: I've told Bob a thousand times, "I know you meant well, but that was one of the schmuckiest things you could have done." There's something about driving on the highway and hearing someone call out, "HEY, UNCLE BOBO-OHHH!" I've heard people yell that when I'm standing on the side of the stage when the Dead come on, I've heard it in restaurants, airports . . .

Nobody I know calls me Uncle Bobo. Nobody! I don't like the name Bill much, either—I was named Wolfgang, and I changed it when I came to America—so I wouldn't mind changing it again.

How about a campaign to *re*-rename me?

◆ ◆ ◆

Bill Graham and Bob Weir were both in attendance in the San Francisco mayor's office on February 25, 1983, for a ceremony announcing Bay Area Music Day. As the ceremony ended and people began to depart, Graham called to Weir and me and gestured for us to follow him.

In the anteroom of the mayor's office, Bill said, "Bob, I want to make you an offer, and I want David to be our witness. Think about this for a while and let me know what you decide.

"I will pay *any price*—money or whatever you want, whatever I have to give you—if you'll take that name off me. *Any price!*"

Weir gave Graham a diabolical smile and said he'd think it over. Nearly two years later, no price has been named, and that nickname continues to dog Bill Graham. From time to time he'll hear "Hey, Uncle Bobo!" in the strangest of places, from the concert halls of San Francisco to the airport in Geneva, Switzerland.

"What do you want me to do
To do for you to see you through?"

PARISH: It's wintertime in New York. We're hopping into a limo on our day off, and this guy hands one of us a shoebox. "Take care of this, man, and don't let him die. Here's the paper on him." It was a lizard, and it came with instructions.

LESH: It was God! And guess what?
GARCIA: We killed him. We fuckin' killed him!
LESH: By accident, of course.
GARCIA: It was pretty fragile. It had to have a certain temperature and all that. Honest to God, they used to rent a room for it and leave it in the bathtub with the hot water sort of dripping.

One day somebody put him in the tub and

"It's hard not to like people who like you." —JERRY GARCIA

STEVE PARISH, EUROPE '72

MARY ANN MAYER

169

turned the hot water on full blast. He meant well . . .

What did you learn from letting the lizard God die?

GARCIA: Not a fuckin' thing.

PARISH: Don't get stuck taking care of the lizard.

GARCIA: That's how easy it is for somebody to sabotage us: They can slip a lizard god to us on the road, and what can we do—give it back? Hell, no! We have to take responsibility for it.

KREUTZMANN: Being in the Grateful Dead is sometimes too much of a responsibility. There are people who expect you to be something when you don't want to be that . . . There's this energy out there, and it's kind of a weird responsibility.

WEIR: What many people fail to recognize is that they are every bit as much a part of the magic as we are. That magic *only* happens when we're on stage performing, and it only happens *between* the band and the audience. It can't be ascribed to any individual, because when he's not performing it's not there.

MARY ANN MAYER

PETER SIMON

DECEMBER 31, 1982, OAKLAND AUDITORIUM. SPEAKERS IN THE LOBBY, HALLWAYS, AND BAR ALLOW THE DANCERS TO FREAK FREELY ALL OVER THE BUILDING.

CHAPTER

14
Band, Crew, and Office

BEEN HERE SO LONG HE'S GOT TO CALLING IT HOME

"There is only one success—to be able to spend your life in your own way."
—CHRISTOPHER MORLEY

"Sure don't know what I'm goin' for
But I'm gonna go for it, for sure"
—"Saint of Circumstance,"
by Bob Weir and John Barlow

"Give me five
I'm still alive
Ain't no luck
I learned to duck"

Just as the music thrives on the tensions among varied styles, so does the Grateful Dead's business organization, a multifarious group made up entirely of people who detest authority and few of whom could describe their jobs in twenty-five words or less. The Grateful Dead has an uncanny ability to balance radically different points of view without collapsing into controversy, and each employee is responsible for his or her own work and its effect on the welfare of the organization.

"This is truly a twenty-four-hour-a-day thing," says Garcia. "It doesn't ever stop, so there's got to be that level of participation, like it or not. Everybody adapts to it as individuals—there's no way you can train somebody for it. It's formless . . . It requires people who are sensitive, who have a sense of humor, and who are a little bit out there—who embrace a little bit of *misfit power*."

Misfit power. Bob Weir coined the phrase to describe the motley array of intellectually bent, cosmically bent, socially bent, motorcyclically bent, and just plain *bent* individuals who comprise the band, crew, and office staff of the Grateful Dead. This community cherishes its diversity and sees the variety of opinions it encompasses as a system of checks and balances which keeps things from going too far in any one direction. Management is a responsibility shared by many men and women, and most business decisions are discussed at company meetings that are held regularly and which are open to *all* employees.

"It's an inefficient organization at times," observes John Barlow, "because there's no hierarchical system keeping the trains running on time.

It's the closest thing to democracy by consensus I've seen, in spite of the fact that there's rarely a consensus."

DAN HEALY [sound engineer]: A consensus is if only half of us are flipping out.

ROBBIE TAYLOR [stage manager]: I've been through a couple of internal upheavals. It's scary: You're on pins and needles, people are yelling and screaming. . . . Some people have to step back a little bit and some people get reprimanded, and everybody learns something about this and that. It's a little scary, but when the dust settles, you know you're alive and you know you're in an organization that can go through those changes—cleaning out the closet, so to speak. I think it's important that these things happen.

HART: Shake the walls of this thing and the bad shit will crumble and the good stuff will stay. Then you'll know what counts, what's worth it.

"Don't tell me this town ain't
got no heart
When I can hear it beat
out loud"

BILL GRAHAM: Ram Rod, Kidd, Parish, and the other [equipment] guys give you the feeling that they don't give a shit. And the great thing about them is that they all *really* give a shit. . . .

Of all the non-musicians in the rock industry, for what he stands for, Ram Rod's got to be number one. He's the quietest leader you'll ever meet. He never gives an order . . . It's just, "Come on. Let's move this thing."

GARCIA: The crew really invented itself. There wasn't a time when any of us in the band *hired* Ram Rod, for example. He was just suddenly there, working [in late 1967, and every step of the way since]. I remember . . . "Who is that again? That guy with the blue eyes who never says anything, that Oregon guy. . . . Oh, yeah, Ram Rod. He's a good guy." However he got in there, he got in there.

So all of a sudden here were these guys. It wasn't like we hired them—they invented themselves, really. Kind of like the band.

It seems as though the crew and sound people are almost full members of the band.

GARCIA: Damn near. They're there when we have our business meetings. We're dragging them

174

PLAYING BASEBALL IN ENGLAND, 1972. *FROM LEFT*: UNIDENTIFIED CREW MEMBER, GRATEFUL DEAD BUSINESS MANAGER DAVID PARKER, BOBBY AT THE BAT, STEVE PARISH ON DECK, CREW MEMBERS REX JACKSON, SONNY HEARD, AND RAM ROD.

MARY ANN MAYER

through life, so why shouldn't they have some say about it?

> "Well, the music's thundering
> Restless and hot
> You keep firin' glances across
> the room"

GARCIA: The crew are on the line when we play, sweating it out like we are, 'cause we go nuts when something goes wrong on stage. It's hairy stuff—every one of us turns into a bug-eyed monster. That's when those guys are really under the gun.

PARISH: You'll be hanging out back there and all of a sudden a noise just rips through you. You know instinctively what it is, just from living with that stuff . . .

GARCIA: It doesn't happen that often, and that's why when it does happen we get pretty unhinged.

> "His brain was boilin'
> His reason was spent"

HARRY POPICK [monitor mixer]: If somebody's growling or exploding because something's wrong, I can't think, "Gee, why is he talking to me like that?" or say, "We're not going to get anywhere this way." I've got to go for the problem.

> "If the thunder don't get you
> Then the lightning will"

PARISH: The bottom line to it all is electricity. We spend many hours with the equipment, but you can never do enough. Electricity is a strange thing; it likes to mess with people. If you *ever* take it for granted—even the smallest cable—it'll catch you. A couple of good shocks and you really get a respect for it. You start learning what you're doing so you can preserve yourself and your friends.

HART: I feel a responsibility to Ram Rod. He hauls my drums all over the country, sets them up—and this is not a glamorous job, man—and

he tears them down and brings them home in as good shape as he took them out. He does this so we're able to be the Grateful Dead. If I didn't give everything I had, I'd be letting Ram Rod down. You couldn't pay him enough . . .

GARCIA: Those guys have to carry all that shit around, and it's a lot of work and a lot of time to spend without any rewards. It's a thankless job.

LESH: They get paid pretty well; I don't think anybody's hurting. But in Jamaica, while we were waiting around for hours and hours so we could go on in the middle of the night—and after all the hassles we had getting that far—Kidd said to me, "I don't get paid enough to do this shit."

Ever wonder why they keep doing it?

GARCIA: I *know* why. They do it because it's what they do. They're in the same boat that we are, in a way.

LESH: It gives their lives meaning, just like it does mine. I don't get paid enough for some of the shit I go through, either, and I wouldn't do it if there wasn't something really special about this.

PARISH: There's an amazing bond that we have.

MONITOR MIXER HARRY POPICK

DAVID GANS

175

We never really understand how strong it is until it's called on, and then it's a really powerful force.

The crew has a group therapy thing that we do. Our people are all really honest with each other. We might do whatever we have to do to get down the road, but we can't lie to each other. After all these years, it'd be useless to lie.

You might have a big fight with a guy, because you're living together in the bus and there are things that happen, but then something will happen during the show and that guy'll be right there, handing you a light or a tool or something.

Plus, you'll be made fun of if you fuck up. That helps keep you on your toes.

RAM ROD: People around here hate fuckin' up the same way twice.

"I said my prayers and went to bed
That's the last they saw of me"

PARISH: Nobody was waking the crew up, so you had to learn to get up by yourself every time

if you didn't want to get left in Nebraska or someplace.

You only have to let that kind of thing happen to you once——

GARCIA: You'd think so [*laughs*].

PARISH: The thing about the road is, some people can adapt to it and some can't. We've had some people come out with us, great geniuses who worked on the PA or whatever, and they just went to pieces.

They tried to replace me once . . . [*leans over and enunciates into the interviewer's microphone*] *They tried to replace me,* and the guy got flaky. That's all—I didn't do anything to him.

"Stranger ones have come by here
Before they flew away"

GARCIA: We got three normal idiots to replace Steve, but no matter how we wired them together they never did go off at the same time.

Steve isn't totally efficient, but there's lots

176

FROM LEFT: FORMER CREW MEMBER JOHN P. HAGEN, RAM ROD, MICKEY HART

BARON WOLMAN

KIDD CANDELARIO, EUROPE '72

ROSIE McGEE ENDE

more levels to him than whether he keeps the equipment in good shape. If I didn't have fundamental faith in Steve, he wouldn't be in the position of responsibility he's in relative to my stuff.

My equipment is a place of real importance, because it can make me really happy and it can also drive me crazy. But it's important to me that the human level be cool, too. I'd rather work on the efficiency of my equipment so there isn't as much to go wrong than have somebody doing it that I didn't like.

"I guess they can't revoke your soul for trying"

PARISH: One time a guy called Jerry and said, "I want to be on the crew. I think I'm right for it."

Jerry told him, "Call Parish. He can probably give you some ideas."

I didn't just hang up on him or laugh it off. I said, "Man, it's a strange thing I can't quite explain. It took years of just hanging out on one level. . . . We were friends, and then these guys taught me . . ."

The guy started crying. I could hear him on the phone, really crying. "C'mon, man, I've got to do this." It was weird.

I said, "If there *was* a test, you just failed it."

About two years later, at Wembley Pool in

"We had everything right yesterday, and then our highly trained and efficient staff came in and changed everything. That's their idea of a cruel little jest." — BOB WEIR

London—it was after the show, and the band had left—this guy came bounding up the steps and said, "Parish! Parish! It's me! I'm the guy who called you. Remember? I cried on the phone and everything!"

I said, "Great. Glad you're here, but get out of the way—we're busy." We were lifting stuff, packing it into cases—totally at the peak of our thing—and this guy got in the way as bad as he

177

THE GRATEFUL DEAD CREW AT WORK, ROTTERDAM, 1972 ·

MARY ANN MAYER

178

could. He had so little idea. It was like walking out and talking to Jerry while he's on stage.

"My work fills the sky with flame"

KREUTZMANN: God threw all these people together: the band, the equipment guys. . . . The Grateful Dead has its own balancing system, its own regulation. There are rules, but they're . . . a deep kind of rules. They're beyond rules; they're life. If you're in this family and you hurt me, you're hurting yourself.

ROCK SCULLY: *Family* is a tricky word to use, and it's used lightly a lot with the Grateful Dead. This is a group of creative individuals getting together for a common cause. It is like a family in the ups and downs. We've come to know and trust each other, and we know we will weather more storms and more good times.

EILEEN LAW: I think that "family" label came from some other people. We're tight, and we all work pretty well, and we're all here for the Grateful Dead.

GARCIA: There's more to life—and to rock and roll, and to our jobs—than just our specific work. That whole "roadie" thing doesn't particularly encourage that, but it's built into our scene because we want there to be more. We're all working on the same thing, so why should we treat each other differently?

Steve's always running little tests on me

[*laughs*]. One time he changed all my strings but one, just to see if I'd notice. I loved that . . .

◆　◆　◆

This road crew doesn't wear matching jumpsuits and scurry around the stage like some technical Tac squad, and they don't hover behind the amp line with freshly tuned guitars at the end of every song. Nobody's job depends on his or her response time, nor do people order each other around.

In fact, the give and take among band and crew would seem to indicate that the musicians serve at the pleasure of the crew. That's because the crew members are the ones who live with the equipment; the stage is more their domain than the players'. And the genuine respect among these people—colleagues, partners, brothers—transcends these harmless incivilities.

And anyway, if the Dead wanted to be treated like stars, would they have a guy like Bill "Kidd" Candelario in their employ?

GARCIA: He could be one of the orneriest guys in the whole wide world.

LESH: Talk about abuse! "Hey, Phil, why don't you drink another gallon of beer, man?"

GARCIA [*laughing*]: The guy is absolutely merciless.

LESH: He's left me dumb so many times, blinking my eyes and flapping my jaws with no sound coming out.

This exchange takes place amid much affectionate laughter, because Kidd is one of these people, a peer. His nasty exoskeleton is a kind of tradition in the Grateful Dead crew, in addition to being part of his Kidd-ness. He's entitled to it.

"Everybody's weird, everybody's bent in the Grateful Dead," Garcia muses. "Nobody is that 'clean,' you know?

"It doesn't ever stop, either. There isn't a moment when suddenly you're okay. There are clearings in the wilderness, and when you get to one you run like hell—but then you're in the jungle again. And everybody has to go through every version of it."

"We've been together all these years," adds Lesh, "and we're *still* goin' through it."

"Searchlight casting
For faults in the clouds of
delusion"

Each member of the Dead party has developed his own way of handling the awesome number and variety of trips laid on them by groupies, dealers, and Deadheads over the years. The combination of general rock and roll insanity and that special Grateful Dead spiritual charisma has attracted every imaginable sob story and con game, and a lifetime of patience could be exhausted in one tour if you're not careful.

LESH: *Not much comin' out of these monitors, Bear.*

[Monitors emit a short, powerful screech.]

LESH: *He wants to show us who's boss, so he sticks a needle into our heads before every performance.*

It's hard to know for certain whether Parish and Kidd and the others developed this yard-dog persona as a result of the years of road games or whether part of their suitability for their jobs comes from a natural ability to intimidate Spamheads and resist the blandishments of would-be pleasure cruisers.

I can't help wond'rin'
Just what you've got
I get the feelin' I'm gonna find
out real soon"

PARISH: A girl pulled up at Front in a BMW with her speakers blaring, hit the brakes, and said, "Hey, what do I have to do to get a pass for the Warfield shows?"

I said, "It's just not like that."

She said, "Come on now—I know there's a price. What do I have to do? Come on, what is it?"

179

People think there's a price they can pay. I've seen people bring all kinds of gifts, and they're the first ones you get rid of later, because they're just obnoxious and they can never change that.

GARCIA: That business of who can be backstage and on stage has been going on since the very beginning. It's one of those things where you have to go on vibes more than anything else.

Those guys go through all the changes. Parish will say, "I'm gonna be a nice guy. I'm never going to throw anybody off the stage or holler at anybody ever again," and then suddenly there'll be forty people up there, bumping into equipment and unplugging things. Then the crew guys go nuts, and they go to the other pole—"Fuck it! Keep everybody off the stage, no matter who they are."

Parish has thrown my *brother* off the stage!

PARISH: You can't give them license up there.

> "Holes in what's left of my
> reason
> Holes in the knees of my blues
> Odds against me been increasin'
> But I'll pull through . . ."

PARISH: It's really an adventurous job in some ways, and an American trip all the way—that carnival thing, packing up and driving somewhere in the middle of the night with all this band's equipment on your back.

KREUTZMANN: When we're on the road, I am so damn proud of this band and all the people who work for us. I'm as proud of our crew as I am of my fellow musicians, and I'll bet there aren't many other bands who feel this way.

ROBBIE TAYLOR: The crew and the sound and lighting people are caring, giving people, and they're *intensely* involved with what's going on. Most of them will go for anything at the last minute, to get it right or to get it weird. That kind of stuff gives me a chill. I love it.

DAN HEALY: For me it's a vehicle that enables people to experiment with musical and technical ideas. It's a workshop and a breadboard as well as a dream and a treat. There's no place in the world I've ever heard of that would deliver the amount of space that this gives me to experiment and try new things—and to hear and appreciate good music.

> "Watch what you hear now
> Make sure it's clear now"

JOHN CUTLER [electronics wizard and recording engineer]: The emphasis here is on quality in all the things we do, and that extends into electronics. I could probably make more money in straight industry, but in industry you do things as cost-effectively as possible. In the Grateful Dead I'm not just allowed, I'm *expected* to use the best parts available and build things as well as I can.

I build equipment that has to stand up on the road, and that's a tall order. I know Weir gets up there and raves about the "crack equipment crew," and my heart does sink when I'm at a show and something breaks down.

◆ ◆ ◆

DAN HEALY AT BERKELEY'S GREEK THEATRE, JULY 1984

DAVID GANS

180

WEIR: [Winterland, December 29, 1977]: Good evening, and welcome to Thursday night at Winterland. We'll be right with you as soon as we make some last-minute adjustments.

We're gonna try to get everything just exactly perfect, on account of our new name is going to be the Just Exactly Perfect Brothers Band.

◆　　◆　　◆

GARCIA: In the Grateful Dead, if you don't have a sense of humor you're screwed.

BARLOW: A couple of years ago I wrote a letter, a "memo to the Californians." It was preachy and sanctimonious, but it was accurate. I had spent some time out there earlier in the year, and it pissed me off because I thought they were all playing a real slack game.

Danny Rifkin [then road manager] needed some time off for some reason, and I think everybody thought it would be a grand prank to expose me to that gig. So I road-managed the "Fifteenth Anniversary" tour in the summer of 1980.

"He thinks he's so smart . . . ?"

BARLOW: Precisely. But they also figured that I could probably do the job. And I could.

It brought me down a couple of notches, because I played a pretty slack game myself.

One of my most strenuous criticisms was that they didn't do what they said they were going to do when they said they were going to do it. I found that happening to me occasionally, just because of the nature of the beast. Being in the belly of the beast made me behave in a way that was in conformity with it. There were a lot of things on that tour that were instructive as hell.

"If I told you 'bout all that went
　　down
It would burn off both your ears"

BARLOW: I've quit . . . and I've had the impulse to quit many times. But one of the things that

181

RECORDING ENGINEER AND ELECTRONICS/COMPUTER WIZARD JOHN CUTLER, LAID BACK IN EGYPT, AUGUST 1978

JERILYN BRANDELIUS

always stopped me was wondering what I'd quit *doing*. Was I going to quit being Weir's friend? Would I just stamp my pretty little foot and say, "I just won't write another song"?

HEALY: If I knew how I got here, maybe I'd know how to quit.

◆　　◆　　◆

If you drew a Grateful Dead corporate flow chart, it would look like an M.C. Escher castle: You can go up the stairs and get to the bottom, and you can go down and end up at the top.

GARCIA: It's like a Möbius strip——

LESH: Möbius Murphy.

RAM ROD: Somebody once asked Steve [Parish], "Who's the boss?" And he said, "The situation is the boss."

"It's got no signs or
dividing lines
And very few rules to guide"

BARLOW: What we've got is something the operation of which we don't understand. If you start fuckin' with the system, changing things around, and introducing new people or new ideas, you don't know what you're going to end up doing. It touches it everywhere, and the whole thing starts rocking. That breeds a certain kind of conservatism. This is a very conservative bunch of people.

HEALY: Your credibility comes from the duration of stickin' with it.

◆　　◆　　◆

The Grateful Dead and these people they're "dragging through life" have made a decision, conscious or otherwise, never to let things get routine—and there's always been a full complement of natural-born boat-rockers on hand to keep things from running too smoothly for too long. They were smart kids to begin with, and they've figured out a way to stay young forever.

They know each other's faults and virtues, and as in a well-weathered marriage, the virtues are often taken for granted while the faults are loudly pointed out from time to time. There are patterns of affection and rage that have been coming and going up to twenty years or more; blind spots, prejudices, and grudges surface periodically and run their course. The consequences are part of the trip because they're part of life, and they help keep the experience pure. As the unfinished Dead song says, "Only the strange remain."

◆　　◆　　◆

What is the Grateful Dead teaching the human race?

LESH: [*Laughs*]

GARCIA: How to fuck up.

PARISH: Don't worry—be happy.

GARCIA: That's it! That's the best thing I've ever heard that anybody should ever hope to want to teach anybody else. That supersedes governments and everything . . . dignity and responsibility to people.

The goal, as far as I'm concerned, is for it to be fun. I've opted for fun in this lifetime.

We're just doing what can be done. We would hope that people will see us as a model—and a lot of people do. It's an approach, really, which could be used in any form.

182

ANDY LEONARD

JOHN BARLOW

"Let your life proceed by its own design"

GARCIA: We abandoned the concept of a game plan early on; as soon as things started happening better than we could plan, we decided to trust that instead.

Seeing as how we're living our life through this medium—"Grateful Deadness," whatever that is—we want it to have as much room as it can possibly have. That means it should be able to incorporate all the shading and changes you can possibly put yourself through. Otherwise, we would be making it too small.

In some ways the whole thing is an act of faith, but somewhere along the line we decided to stick it out past what would normally have been discouraging experiences. It's had enough encouraging input to nurture it, or at least to let us have faith in it.

If this ever lets us down, fuck it—we've had a good ride, and now it's back to the gas station.

There's a lesson to be learned: If you're able to enjoy something, to devote your life to it . . . it will work out for you. I think it has something to do with whether or not you have sufficient faith in the vehicle.

LESH: If people watch us doing things together well, it might dawn upon them that they themselves can get together and do something, whatever it may be.

I may get bored with the Grateful Dead from time to time, but I never get bored with being in the Grateful Dead. To me, the Grateful Dead is life—the life of the spirit and the life of the mind, as opposed to standing in line and marking time in the twentieth century. —PHIL LESH

It's a lifestyle and a life work. I've really come to accept that; it was a joke at first. We were going to stick 'em with the shit and split, but it got serious right away. I said, "I don't want to be doing this when I'm thirty," because at first I didn't realize it could be art.

When did you decide it could?

LESH: Oh, about two weeks after we got into it.

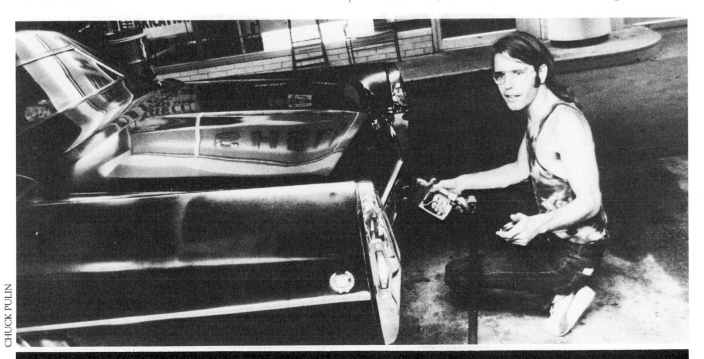

WEIR GASSES UP THE DEAD'S LIMO EN ROUTE TO A GIG AT YALE BOWL, NEW HAVEN, CONNECTICUT, JULY 1971.

CHUCK PULIN

183

184

GARCIA: People say, "Aren't you surprised you've been together for twenty years?" I keep saying it's like we're just getting started. There's so much we haven't even done with the band in its present incarnation, places we've touched on imperfectly in other forms . . .

HART: It's a band of imperfect people playing imperfect music, but with a certain kind of spirit.

LESH: Nobody ever gets exactly what he wants from the Grateful Dead.

The Dead have been called "America's longest-running musical argument——

LESH: A verbal argument has two sides, but a musical argument makes the two sides one thing, like counterpoint. A fugue or a sonata movement takes two or more different ideas and shows how they relate to each other. A musical argument is something that keeps going; you uncover new details and new combinations. Let's call it "conversation."

◆   ◆   ◆

Art created by committee can be an ugly proposition, and the constant compromising makes the Dead a yin-yang situation. Imagine playing in a band of brawling brothers who'll break your heart by design or by accident one moment and then crown your very existence eight bars later. "I wouldn't want it to have any less range than that," Garcia has confessed. "If it did, we'd be cutting it off somewhere short of its full capacity as an experience.

"We're frequently seen as being privileged somehow, but being in the Grateful Dead doesn't exempt you from anything, particularly, and the reward is fleeting. Everything we've done is culminated in the last note we played. If it was a bad gig, it's as if the only reasonable thing to do is end it all.

"The hope that it'll change for the better is ever-present, and it happens enough that things aren't completely dark. But it's balanced on the most recent experience: No matter how good it's ever been, if the last gig was a bum one, you're stuck."

◆　　◆　　◆

HUNTER: We're for ourselves more than anything else—for our own musical development. If it goes through a slump, it goes through a slump. But I think we've made a career out of meeting different expectations than were had of us.

GARCIA: There are people older than us still playing, like Willie Nelson, Waylon Jennings, the Rolling Stones, who use rock-sounding instrumentation. With us, though, it's not necessarily rock and roll, or "youthful" music. That

ROBERT HUNTER

doesn't define what we're all about. Egypt, for example, was no money-making venture. It was a folly, but to us it was worth it. That kind of stuff is what we're about.

HART: As long as I can breathe, and as long as we can play together and have fun, we'll grow old with the music and the music will grow old with us. There's no reason why we can't play until we drop. That'd be a good way of going—I'd rather do that than drop in front of a TV set drinkin' beer.

Anyway, this music is medicine. It makes me young. It *feels* young, real good.

"There's a lot of whimsicality in this organization. If we could get a spot for the Grateful Dead on the space shuttle, I'm sure we'd try for it. First concert in space! —JOHN BARLOW

If I'm still alive and the Grateful Dead are still alive [at fifty], you bet I'll still be doing it. Why not? Look at Basie and Ellington—they kept at it and their music changed, but they stayed musically viable. There's no reason in the world the Grateful Dead can't go on for years.

WEIR: If the Grateful Dead continues just the way we have—assuming we all live for a while—we're guaranteed a living. Beyond that, what more do you want?

"Unbroken chain, sorrow and
　　　pearls . . ."

The Grateful Dead built their music and their, uh, lifestyle honestly in a time when it was possible to do so. They became a band under different circumstances and with different goals from most rock musicians, and they've gotten along just fine without having to answer to any authorities higher than themselves—and they've stayed pretty high over the years.

The musical influences at work in the Grateful Dead—and the personalities and tastes—could hardly be more diverse. They've synthesized a

185

weirdly pantheistic music and with it a lifestyle that demands complete surrender and yet affords a great amount of individual freedom. It's the ongoing acceptance and optimism of each participant—the knowledge that if it doesn't work out today it might pay off tomorrow—that sustains the Grateful Dead and their fans.

◆　　◆　　◆

GARCIA: It's really difficult to extrapolate from the Grateful Dead to the music business. We're not quite in that world as it's presently constructed—we're like the exception to every rule. We're in some kind of non-formula, non-linear development path, and it's definitely *growing*. It's not like we're just dragging along the same audience—we're actually getting new people.

I think that as an idea, we're *still* a little too radical for a lot of places. But people catch on to us pretty quick, and I don't think we're very frightening. In most places, when the cops and security people experience our audience and find that they're pretty nice people, they take to us. The world . . . kind of likes us better than it used to. Our audience isn't destructive.

People react weirdly at first, especially if it's a big show. They get scared because of all those people camping out downtown. It looks funny, you know . . .

There's parts of the world we can't go to, because I think we would represent a little too much chaos . . .

We're sort of parallel with the world, kind of skipping and slithering along while the rest of the world is grinding along. Sometimes we're a couple of years ahead, and sometimes we're a couple of years behind. But it's definitely at our own rate, and it doesn't rely on what's happening in the big world.

WEIR: We've created our own little place to be in this world, and we're doing well enough.

LESH: Mostly out of sheer luck and random facility . . .

WEIR: Dogged persistence, and more good times than bad times.

LESH: I'm so glad it's still going on, because I know we're not finished with it yet. There's still plenty to be done. The great thing is that it has some kind of an audience.

WEIR: For those who are drawn into whatever it is we do, through whatever avenues or for whatever reasons, we can and do supply a little genuine joy. I don't know if that's a complete reason for being, either for me personally or for the band, but it's a good holding pattern . . . until we figure out if there's something more to go for.

Making magic with the rest of the band is, number one, how I've always made my living, and, number two, how I've always received my greatest gratification.

If art can serve to further civilization, then it's performing its ultimate goal. If it makes you get up in the morning feeling that maybe you can punch it out with the social order and the situation you've been force-fed until that morning, then that's wonderful. . . .

187

"Oh, well, a touch of grey
Kinda suits you anyway"

GARCIA: It's been truly fantastic.

LESH: Yeah, beyond our wildest dreams.

You never had any expectations? You just fell into this?

GARCIA: Hopes, yes, but never this. We were looking for good times, really, but extra special good times with a capital G.T. *our* kind of good times: good and weird.

"Old men sing about their
　　dreams
Women laugh and children
　　scream
And the band keeps playing on"

CHAPTER 15
Epilogue

AND NO ONE KNOWS MUCH MORE OF THIS THAN ANYONE HAS SEEN

This book was originally published in 1985, the year the Grateful Dead celebrated the twentieth anniversary of their first gig with Phil Lesh on electric bass. Publication of this new edition marks the end of the Grateful Dead as a performing unit.

Jerry Garcia died of a heart attack on August 9, 1995. He was in a rehabilitation facility near his home, trying to get clean after years of addiction to heroin. His last recording session had been just a few days earlier, recording Jimmie Rodgers's "Blue Yodel #9" with David Grisman for a tribute album being assembled by Bob Dylan.

BOB WEIR: He had seen a few doctors with regard to his health, and had come up with a plan. First things first, he was going to try to free himself of his drug dependency. Then he was going to try to engineer a program to bring his body around. He went down swinging: He was involved in trying to get himself healthy. He was maybe a bit too ambitious about it, and his body wasn't up to the strain.

MICKEY HART: It was a shock. We never really turned the page—the page was turned for us.

There were a lot of dark marks on Garcia's life, but the note, the sound, was pure. It came from a pure space, and he goes back to that pure space now. His life was well spent, you know. It couldn't have been spent better.

◆　　◆　　◆

In December of 1995, the remaining band members announced that they would never again perform as the Grateful Dead. The *San Francisco Chronicle* reported that it was drummer Bill Kreutzmann who retired, effectively deciding the matter, but Lesh, Hart, and Weir all insisted that it was a mutual decision by the five surviving members.

HART: It was in everybody's gut, wondering what it would be like without Jerry. [Grateful Dead music] was a conversation between people, and when you lose one of your main guys, it breaks up the intimate conversation—*and* this love affair that we were having with the audience. Jerry was a big part of that. Garcia was a habit! You gotta have it, and it's really hard to let go of something you gotta have. You want to hold on to it 'cause it was so great, but we could never have done it better. We thought it should go out with dignity.

HERB GREENE

JERRY GARCIA AND PHIL LESH, 1987

190

WEIR: I tend to take death fairly matter-of-factly. There is absolutely nothing you can do about it. I try to be strong for people who are more emotional about it. On the other hand, for what it's worth, Jerry was pretty much my best friend, so it's not a particularly easy loss for me. But I have a torch to carry here; to spend a lot of time moping and grieving seems way beside the point to me. I'm doing what I believe he would have me doing: bringing music to people.

LESH: We're looking into the possibility of creating some kind of gathering place, perhaps to be called Terrapin Station, with a performance space and Virtual Reality rooms, hopefully with Grateful Dead music and/or videos playing all the time. We want to have a place where Deadheads can come and recapture as much of that spirit as possible without actually having a live performance.

WEIR: The sense of community is one of the most resplendent gems in the Grateful Dead crown. For music to bring people together is the most important thing the Grateful Dead has had to offer over the years.

◆　　◆　　◆

"And it's one in ten thousand
that come for the show"

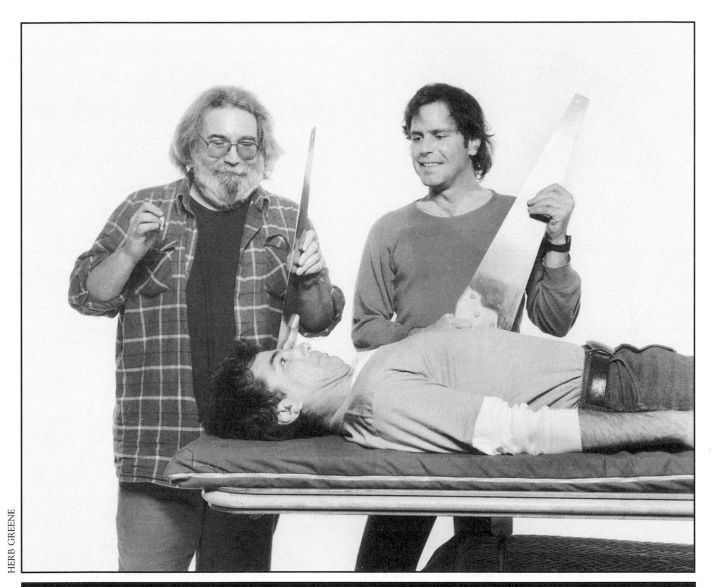

JERRY GARCIA AND BOB WEIR PREPARE TO COMMIT "TRUE ROAD SURGERY" ON MICKEY HART, 1987

The summer of 1985 was a busy and musically exciting season for the Dead, and the twentieth-anniversary news hook got them some major coverage in the mainstream media. Network newsmagazine cameras lingered on the tie-dyed, sun-baked psychedelic sideshow that accompanied the band on tour before turning to the increasingly bemused and ever-charismatic Jerry Garcia for a characteristically self-effacing remark about the inexplicability of the band's enduring fame.

For longtime fans, the Grateful Dead was an ongoing commitment. This music was not hormonal and *immediate* the way rock 'n' roll was before the Beatles took the genre from teenage to adulthood,

broadening their musical and thematic range with every new recording. The Dead started out with an appreciation of history, drawing from a century's worth of popular music forms as well as older classical influences. Living in the moment and enjoying life today was very definitely central to the hippie ethic that the Dead embodied, but "Hope I die before I get old" was not a sustainable philosophy and everybody knew it.

Grateful Dead music is for people who have lived some; it's music that you live *with*. Grateful Dead songs don't yield up their whole meaning in one listen: Every Dead performance is subject to interpretation by the performer, by the rest of the band,

JON SIEVERT

JERRY GARCIA AND HIS OLD FRIEND DAVID GRISMAN REUNITED IN 1990 FOR A SERIES OF ACOUSTIC PERFORMANCES AND RECORDINGS THAT REPRESENT GARCIA'S BEST WORK IN THE LAST FIVE YEARS OF HIS LIFE. TWO ALBUMS ON GRISMAN'S ACOUSTIC DISC LABEL—*JERRY GARCIA/DAVID GRISMAN* (1990) AND *NOT FOR KIDS ONLY* (1993) HAVE BEEN RELEASED FROM SOME FORTY DIFFERENT RECORDING SESSIONS WITH VARIOUS GROUPS OF PLAYERS.

and by the audience. For the long-term Deadhead, every encounter with Grateful Dead music can be a reckoning of sorts—a music history lesson, or a trip to the far reaches of consciousness, or a plunge to the depths of the soul.

HART: There was a trance-inducing element in our music. These weren't five-minute grooves—there were 20-, 30-, 40-, 50-minute grooves. We played for many hours. That allowed for a certain kind of group rapture that you couldn't get from American Bandstand.

There was an improvisational nature to the music that was a model for other people to emulate. There was a certain freedom that we brought to the music, that fed the music and made it strong. There was a circus-like atmosphere, the freedom of personal expression; the dance, the twirling—the

dervish-like performance of the people that were responding to the music. People forgot themselves, and started going into other realms of consciousness—which is what the Grateful Dead was all about: We were headed into the zone. We weren't trying to entertain as much as to transport.

JOHN PERRY BARLOW: The Grateful Dead as a musical ecosystem has been incredibly inclusive. From the beginning, the Grateful Dead was this great stew pot in which you could pour everything from reggae to zydeco to, you know, the throat-singers of Tuva, and have it all come out in some kind of more or less culturally comprehensible format—partly because Grateful Dead songs, as Ornette Coleman once said, are amazingly simple at the start.

I'm a great believer in the idea of hybrid vigor: That a certain kind of judicious mongrelization is how life proceeds, how it fights against the forces of entropy and makes itself more complex and more energetic and more useful.

◆　◆　◆

How did the Grateful Dead change the world?
CAROLYN GARCIA: I think everybody of a certain age—anybody with any spunk, anyway—considers that they see the possibilities of changing things. That was a given. The reason it seemed possible was that so little else seemed to be happening in the United States. It was a very bland place in 1964. No one at that time had much information about other possibilities besides the way America was.

The Vietnam War was a huge part of this stuff.

To make yourself unattractive to the draft was important! [laughs]

ALAN TRIST, (Ice Nine Publishing): The multiple energies of the sixties, directing consciousness away from the pit of dull materialism and newfound warmongering and towards the spirit of creativity, cooperation, peace, and love, changed the world. The Grateful Dead was one node of this seminal era, but their phenomenal long-lastingness and stalwart fans, yea even unto the mid-nineties, provided a continuity to that message and, to the chagrin of social forces of shriveled sobriety, wouldn't let it die. The rest will be history.

The nub of this process was, of course, the songs, the music, the concerts, the dance, the fair, the celebration, the festival, the road tour, the parking lot, the X-factor, etc., and its wheel is the community,

193

JON SIEVERT

GARCIA BACKSTAGE AT SQUAW VALLEY, AUGUST 1991. HE PLAYED WITH GRISMAN AND WITH THE JERRY GARCIA BAND THAT WEEKEND.

built from these ingredients, which now exists in joyful nooks and crannies throughout society.

GARY LAMBERT (editor of the *Grateful Dead Almanac*): They played free improvised music to more people than anyone ever in history, and they showed that an improvised way of doing business, of conducting your life, can be highly successful. I think they inspired a lot of people to try that in their own lives.

STEVE SILBERMAN (author of *Skeleton Key: A Dictionary for Deadheads*): The Dead and Deadheads put up a Big Tent where it was all right to *play* with the spontaneous heart of a child; to check your hangups at the door; to offer up your body as a vehicle of ecstasy; and face the unmediated bliss and terror of existence without illusions, in a place that felt completely safe. Then they took it on the road, so millions of people could taste that gloriously subversive possibility—and they kept it rolling for thirty years.

CAROLYN GARCIA: There was a long period of non-success, when nobody came, or bought any re-

cords. But the alternative community was developing during that period, and that took a long time to build up.

And the idea was to recruit people for that?

CAROLYN GARCIA: Yes, I do think that the idea was to recruit people for that. There was no plan to take responsibility for them or to tell them what to do, but merely to help them open to some of the possibilities that life has.

JOHN DWORK (editor of *Dupree's Diamond News*): The Grateful Dead experience reminded a new generation of the role that tribalism, ecstasy, a sense of adventure, and an eagerness to explore the unknown can play in striving for a balanced, prosperous life.

STEVE BROWN (filmmaker): They gave people a spiritual type of exercise that they could do to music, which I found to be one of the more refreshing things that people could experience together. You got to go out and exercise your soul every time they came to town.

GERRIT GRAHAM (actor): I think they provided

GRATEFUL DEAD PERFORM FOR 90,000 PEOPLE AT JFK STADIUM IN PHILADELPHIA, JULY 10, 1987.

HERB GREENE

THE DEAD WITH BOB DYLAN, MARCH 1987.

195

community and a sense of belonging. As banal as it is to say that, it's very difficult to find that in a life whose hallmarks, increasingly, are isolation and alienation and deracination and disinclusion. The Dead included us in their trip. They weren't above us, they weren't better than us—in a funny way they *were* us. We were all on the bus together.

SENATOR PATRICK LEAHY (D-VT): With some, following the Dead around became their life. I'm not sure they were the majority by any means. I think a lot of people found that their life was improved—not in the sense that you learn a new lan-

guage or something, but you felt better. The world stopped for a little bit while you realized that maybe the rest of the world moves too fast and it's time to stop and take stock. At least that's the way I always felt.

"The Grateful Dead reinforced my suspicions that we are all one."
—GOLDIE RUSH, *member,* Ship of Fools *Steering Committee*

Sitting on an upturned trunk on stage beside the sound mixer at the Grateful Dead concert is about as far removed as you can be from debating an issue on the floor of the United States Senate. [laughs] I know it helped me, because I found I usually came back and looked at things anew—once my ears stopped ringing.

NATALIE DAVIS-CONNOLLY (journalist): The first time I saw them was in 1980. I was going to school at the University of Maryland in College Park, right outside of DC. It was a novelty for me because they were playing at the Baltimore Civic Center, and I was from Baltimore. It was cool to go to Baltimore without telling my folks.

I remember going up to the old civic center, a cement building where they used to have hockey and b-ball games. A warhorse of a building, very functional. Nothing artistic about it at all. I had been there a million times, for the Ice Capades, the Jackson Five, all sorts of things.

I walked in there, and I could not believe what I had found. I had been in a world where most people were nasty and mean and judgmental and cruel, and prepared to think ill of you just by taking a look at you. Here you could walk into this world and the assumption was to love you. It blew my mind; to this day it blows my mind. Everyone was valuable, and everyone had something that they could add to the party to make it richer. That was really cool. I suppose that's what kept me—in addition to the music—enthralled for sixteen years now. Absolutely enthralled. I travel in a lot of different circles; my work allows me to do a lot of different things and talk to a lot of different people. Bar none, the best people are Deadheads.

SALLY MULVEY (publisher of *Dupree's Diamond News*): It was a very cool scene when I was fourteen. It was safe and fun and exciting, and everybody looked out for everybody. It was like summer camp for four hours: You were brought into a space with people from who-knows-where, but it was a protected space where you didn't have to worry about how you were acting.

◆   ◆   ◆

For a musical historian, or even for a DJ just trying to mix up the tunes and jams for a weekly radio

"They gave us a positive ritual. This was one of the few places where people could gather together and nobody was against anything. Everybody was there for something, and that's pretty cool."
—SUSAN MILLMAN, *photographer*

hour, the Dead presented some problems, even at their best. Vocal weakness, weird mixes, sloppy transitions, etc.—the emphasis on novelty tended to work against polish and consistency. But perfection and repeatability were not a core value of Grateful Dead music.

As rich with nuances, superstitions, and traditions as a baseball game, the Dead culture was mainstream enough (by which I mean it generated enough action in the sea of capital) to provide the economic basis for the social construct, but also weird enough to attract the alien and the alienated. By entwining our lives with this music over the years, we became entwined in the lives of the musicians. For many people, being a Deadhead was more than just loving the music.

In August of 1986, Garcia fell ill. Fans were gathering at the Ventura County Fairgrounds in southern California when the news hit: Jerry was in a diabetic coma, complicated by an abscessed tooth, and would not be playing that day, nor any time soon. Word spread rapidly via mainstream news media and the Deadhead community's vast commercial and social network.

In the fledgling Grateful Dead conference in The Well (an early outpost on what is now known as the Internet), the Deadheads shared information as it came in. One community member transcribed an announcement by publicist Dennis McNally that he'd heard on the radio, and another offered information on diabetes and how Garcia's dental problems exacerbated the situation. The diagnosis prompted some comic relief about renaming songs ("Saccharine Magnolia"?), and many people offered prayers and other messages of spiritual support. Rumors were vetted and reliable information was propagated.

Online talk of a benefit concert to raise money for the Dead soon turned to the more realistic idea of a "virtual Grateful Dead concert" where the community could gather, listen to music, sell their wares, and send healing thoughts Garciaward. And such events did take place in many locations. In San Francisco, it was "Night of the Living Deadheads," featuring live music by Dead cover bands, a vending area, and viewing of a videotaped interview with the recuperating Garcia. United by concern for the health of our beloved bandleader, the community discovered that it could cohere even without regular large-scale get-togethers. And the online community of Deadheads has continued to grow and thrive, stoked with information and opinion, making new human connections every minute of every day.

"This event was a rehearsal for Jerry's death and the end," recalled author Steve Silberman. "People had a reckoning of what the Dead meant to them, for their lives—and when the boys came back, at least some of the mega-momentum came from the fact that we had all tasted the end—of the music, of Jerry, and of our community."

LYRICISTS ROBERT HUNTER (LEFT) AND JOHN BARLOW, 1987.

HERB GREENE

The Dead's career did kick into high gear after Garcia returned to performing in December 1986, starting with a few acoustic shows and several gigs with the Jerry Garcia Band at the Stone in San Francisco.

The Dead returned to the stage with three nights at the 15,000-seat Oakland Coliseum Arena. There were many emotional moments in that first show, December 15, starting with first-set opener, "Touch of Grey," whose optimistic chorus was given an especially joyous literal interpretation: "I will get by/I will survive." The last verse of "Candyman" provided another catharsis: As Garcia sang "Hand me my old guitar," the crowd began to cheer; then he sang "Pass the whiskey 'round" and the audience rose in expectation and exploded as he sang the next lines: "Won't you tell everybody you meet/ That the candyman's in town." The bridge of "Wharf Rat" took on extra poignancy: "I'll get a new start/Live the life I should," followed by the uplifting "I'll get up and fly away" refrain and a soaring instrumental passage that reached into every attending heart with the news that the story would continue.

Although the band performed in relatively intimate venues such as the Henry J. Kaiser Convention Center, Stanford University's Frost Amphitheater and the Greek Theater in Berkeley between New Year's 1986 and the summer of 1989, outside the Bay Area the days of Grateful Dead concerts in intimate halls were over.

The post-meltdown year was a period of intense creativity for Garcia and his bandmates. Garcia did a run on Broadway, at the Lunt-Fontanne Theater, with the Jerry Garcia Band and the Jerry Garcia Acoustic Band, featuring longtime pals Sandy Rothman (mandolin, dobro, vocals) and David Nelson (guitar, vocals), along with fiddler Kenny Kosek and the rhythm section from the electric band.

In 1987 the Grateful Dead finally got into the studio to record *In the Dark*, which included several songs that had been in the band's live repertoire for most of the eighties. To the astonishment of just about everybody, the album was a bona fide hit, propelled by the opening track, "Touch of Grey." The band made videos for "Touch of Grey," "Hell in a Bucket," and the pointedly political Weir-Barlow

197

composition "Throwing Stones." It was "a very happy time," Mountain Girl recalled. "Doing those videos was just a gas for Jerry." Garcia and longtime video collaborator Len Dell'Amico completed *So Far,* an hour-long video that combined live-action performance footage with montages of real and computer-generated images.

Nineteen eighty-seven also saw the teaming of Bob Dylan and the Grateful Dead. Rehearsals took place at the Dead's studio in San Rafael in the spring, and the band backed Dylan in six shows spread out among dates on the Dead's summer tour from July 4 to July 26. A live album, *Dylan and the Dead,* was released early in 1989, produced by Jerry Garcia and John Cutler.

One interesting side effect of the Dylan-Dead collaboration was a collaboration between Dylan and Robert Hunter. Dylan flipped through a book of new Hunter lyrics at Club Front, Hunter recalled, "liked these tunes, put 'em in his pocket, went off, set 'em to music, recorded 'em, and—first time I met him he said, 'Hey, I just recorded two of your tunes.'

"And I said, 'Neat!' Hunter laughed. He didn't even ask first? "Bob Dylan doesn't have to ask a lyricist if he can do his tunes," Hunter replied. Come *on,* man!"

The songs—"Silvio" (with Garcia, Weir, and Mydland adding vocals) and "The Ugliest Girl in the World"—appear on Dylan's 1988 album *Down in the Groove.*

"I've got to say this for the record," Hunter added. "You've got your Grammys, you've got your Bammies [Bay Area Music Awards], you've got your Rock 'n' Roll Hall of Fame. As far as I'm concerned, Bob Dylan has done two of my songs, and those other things sound far away, distant, and not very interesting."

> "Thought I heard a blackbird singin'
> up on Bluebird Hill"

Around the time of the Dylan-Dead tour, Bob Bralove was brought aboard to bring computer-assisted MIDI (Musical Instrument Digital Interface) technology to all the players. With special pickups in their guitars, Lesh and Weir and Garcia now had access to the same array of synthesized and sampled "real" sounds that the keyboardists and drummers had been using for years. Garcia, who had often described his playing in terms of other instruments he heard in his mind's ear, now began to play flutes, cornets, mutated double-reeds, and some seriously bizarre sounds (one musician described one of them as "like he's hitting a parking meter with a lead pipe") regularly. And the second set "space" jams became even more sonically adventurous.

SILBERMAN: MIDI allowed the Dead to become what they had always aimed to be—the Planet Earth Rock 'n' Roll Orchestra, adding voices from any culture, any instrument, even non-musical textures, to create a spontaneous landscape of sounds drawn from all realms of human experience. This was a time when space could incorporate traditional instruments from the rainforest, Chinese and Bal-

JON SIEVERT

STEVE PARISH KEEPS AN EYE ON JERRY'S GEAR
WHILE THE BAND PLAYS, 1988.

inese metallophones, talking drums and kalimbas, hip-hop-esque tape loops, and even entire orchestras playing chords from "The Rite of Spring." The Dead at this juncture were the hugest realization of the impulse behind Varèse's "Ionisation" and the twentieth-century notion that *any* sound in the composer's universe be available as a compositional element. And they were playing this in sports arenas! So what if some kids went to the bathroom—others heard it for what it was. Roll over Schönberg, tell Bartok the news.

◆　◆　◆

"The singing man is at his song
The holy on their knees
The reckless are out wrecking
The timid plead their pleas"

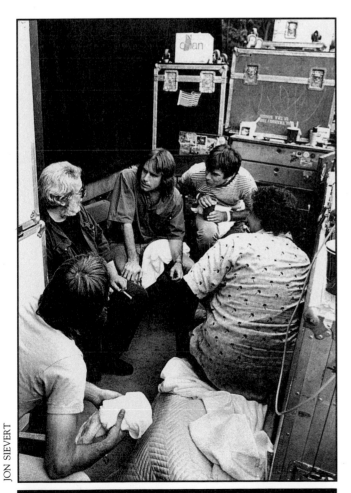

JON SIEVERT

JUST BEFORE THE SECOND SET, APRIL 30, 1988 AT STANFORD UNIVERSITY'S FROST AMPHITHEATER.

What happened to the Dead in the last half of the eighties was what happened to the Haight-Ashbury in 1967: Images of unsupervised fun and open-hearted community drew thousands of new fans into the scene, and as the Jubilee expanded it became harder and harder for the music to remain at the hub of the culture. The parking lot became a destination in its own right, with traveling merchants and freeloaders touring along with the band and the fans, and local thrill-seekers and opportunists showing up to hang out. The band's prosperity put them in larger facilities, and the scene outside the concert grew and grew.

REBECCA ADAMS (sociologist): My hunch is that if the Dead hadn't continued playing, a lot of what started in the sixties would have stopped right there. They kind of dragged the sixties forward through the Reagan and Bush years, and I'm not sure that would have happened without them—even for people who weren't Deadheads.

BLAIR JACKSON: All through the seventies and early eighties the Grateful Dead kept that sixties spirit alive. I guess you could say they were a traveling museum, a living exhibit of the sixties in a way. Some people think it's a throwback, but I always thought it was the evolution of what it was, and since the essence of it didn't change from the mid-sixties all the way into the nineties, you could sort of glom onto it at any point and it would still have that sixties essence—which was appealing to a lot of people. It didn't necessarily mean we're not living in today—it meant, *this is the way we're living today*.

They legitimized that, in a way, by being really successful. For all the problems that the mega-Dead period brought with it, with the vendors and all that, it brought back that sixties thing of feeling that you didn't have to live within the system. In the sixties, there was cheap rent everywhere; people were living together communally; you could essentially drop out. What the whole mega-Dead scene provided was another way you could drop out. It might not have had the same sort of heavy philosophical underpinnings that it did for a lot of people in the sixties, but there were also a lot of people in the sixties who dropped out just because they didn't want to live in the straight world. That's what the

199

Grateful Dead provided for a lot of people in the eighties and nineties.

GARY LAMBERT: My feeling has always been that a lot of the more clueless Heads were a pretty direct product of the mass media's cluelessness about the Dead. Think about it—whenever there was press on the Dead, what was the focus? Sixties, hippies, tie-dye, drugs—elements that were part of the Grateful Dead gestalt, to be sure, but hardly the whole picture. The local TV station would go down to a show, set up on the outer fringes of the parking lot, and stick a camera into the face of the person who most fit their incredibly narrow profile of a "hippie"—get a few shots of kids smoking, panhandling, suckin' on balloons, back to the studio, cut a quick tease—"The Grateful Dead bring the sixties to Akron: film at eleven." Just right for getting the local authorities into a lather, but also something that'll look real good to a teenage misfit without much goin' on in his life—"Hey, people hangin' out, doin' dope, drinkin' beer, fuckin' off? That's for me!"

Much like *Time* magazine's incredibly superficial hippie issue and that ridiculous CBS news report helped get the Haight overrun in 1967, so this absurd media focus on surface elements of the Dead scene brought around all sorts of people who wanted to play at being Deadheads without understanding the larger social context or the concept of cooperation and interdependence that the scene needed to keep running smoothly.

◆　　◆　　◆

PHIL LESH, 1995.

BILL SMYTHE

The economy—both official and unofficial—underlying the Grateful Dead culture continued to burgeon throughout the band's final decade. Grateful Dead Mercantile was formed to handle their licensing and merchandising operations, making deals with inspired Deadhead craftspeople as well as major corporate vendors; the *Grateful Dead Almanac*, a quarterly newsletter/catalog, began publication in the fall of 1994, with Gary Lambert at the helm; Grateful Dead ticket sales, instituted in the early eighties in an effort to assure that concert tickets went to devoted fans rather than scalpers, controlled approximately half of the available seats and employed several dozen of those very fans. Orders in elaborately-decorated envelopes were part of the fun for the ticket office staff, and the seasonal ritual of filling out three-by-five cards and postal money orders was a big part of Deadhead life—an improvement over the vagaries of lining up for tickets at electronic ticket agencies in shopping malls and record stores.

I wandered into a local radio station in San Francisco to promote *Playing in the Band*, got interested in radio production, and wound up launching a nationally syndicated weekly radio show, "The Grateful Dead Hour," that still airs weekly ten years later.

> "Do everything that's in you
> You feel to be your part"

Along the way the Dead conspired with some friends to form the Rex Foundation, formalizing their career-long tradition of giving away large amounts of money earned from their performances. With promoter Bill Graham, basketball hero Bill Walton, Alabama oral surgeon and longtime Dead pal Bernie Bildman, and several band members on board, the Rex Foundation maintained an overhead as close to zero as possible and gave away millions of dollars over the last decade or so of the Dead's existence. Characteristically, this was done with no public fanfare whatsoever, and with no strings attached. Most of the money was given to small-scale, direct-action humanitarian endeavors; some went to musical projects, such as the effort to record a major work by obscure British composer Havergal Brian.

The Dead did make some higher-profile appearances on behalf of causes, including a massive 1988 benefit for the Rainforest Action Network, Greenpeace, and related endeavors. Members of the band testified before Congress about environmental issues on at least one occasion.

For the first decade or so of the Rex Foundation's existence, the band dedicated one run of shows per year—often a three-show engagement at the delightful Cal Expo in Sacramento—to the Rex Foundation. Band and promoter donated all profits to Rex, and booth space was made available for beneficiaries to present information to the fans. In the last few years of the band's existence, they began scheduling Rex benefits in other cities on the tour; efforts were made to distribute funds in the area of each benefit show. The wealth was most definitely shared.

◆　　◆　　◆

Bob Weir and his sister Wendy collaborated on a pair of children's books, *Panther Dream* (1991) and *Baru Bay: Australia* (1995). Wendy did the illustrations, and Bob narrated and composed music for the audio version that accompanied the books.

Why have you chosen the children's book as your vehicle for getting this environmental message across?

BOB WEIR: We're looking at getting a crack at their young, fresh minds, you know, and instilling a sense of appreciation of nature and environment that might stick with them. The planet's going to hell in a handbasket, and they're the folks that can turn it around if there's anything left—if we give them anything to go on.

WENDY WEIR: Young children have a natural love of nature and the environment and a reverence for what's around them. It's only as they get older that they lose this appreciation. So if you reinforce it at a young age and work with their imagination, and tell them that this is the way it really is, then they're going to continue to reinforce that as they grow older and really respect the environment and take care of it.

BOB WEIR: Things like greed and arrogance and self-servingness will tend to occlude your senses of joy and wonderment if you let them. But if we can stoke those senses of joy and wonderment enough,

201

BOB WEIR, JERRY GARCIA, AND STEVE PARISH, NOVEMBER 1991.

HERB GREENE

then maybe it's going to be hard for the other stuff that comes as you get older to overcome the original joy.

WENDY WEIR: And the other thing is that parents will listen to their children. So if they see their children having an incredible experience, it will open them up more. It helps break down their structure, and they can become more childlike.

◆　　◆　　◆

The post-meltdown years saw a creative renaissance in the Grateful Dead as a musical ensemble. Although *Built to Last*, their 1989 studio album, failed to reach the creative and commercial heights of its predecessor, the material written for the album worked just fine in concert. Revivified by Garcia's recovery and armed with immense new computer-assisted sonic palettes, the group mind soared to heights unseen since the early seventies.

STEVE SILBERMAN: I'll never forget coming home to a dozen messages on my answering machine, the night of October 9, 1989. "Steve, you're not going to *believe* this. Are you sitting down?"

The long and the short of it was that the "Formerly the Warlocks" show [an unannounced performance at the Coliseum in Hampton, Virginia] had been more than a stealth gig, but a revival, not only of "Dark Star" and "Attics of My Life," but of the band's ability to *astound* its audience by playing huge long-form jams that reached way back to the roots of the Dead's own mission and history. All the shows that month were spectacular, culminating in the half-hour excursion in Miami from "Dark Star" to points unknown, where a bassoon could discourse with kalimbas and typewriters, and the music transcended even its own goofy, open-ended genre to become a truly majestic world music. You can hear that energy in the "Eyes of the World" with Branford Marsalis [March 29, 1990 at the Nassau Coliseum in Uniondale, New York, released on the 1990 live album *Without a Net*], when the soloists drew on any sound imaginable to further the conversation.

◆　　◆　　◆

On July 26, 1990, three days after the end of the summer tour, keyboardist Brent Mydland died from an overdose of cocaine and heroin. *Without a Net* is dedicated to "Clifton Hanger," which was the road name Mydland used to keep from being bothered with phone calls while on tour.

The band lost little time, thanks to Bruce Hornsby, a Virginian who grew up playing in Dead cover bands and was a successful and well-respected recording artist in his own right (he won a Grammy for "Best New Artist" of 1986 and made the charts with a succession of singles starting with "The Way It Is"). Hornsby had sat in with the Dead a few times when his band, the Range, had shared bills with them. Hornsby agreed to fill in on keyboards so the band could continue touring while a permanent replacement was brought up to speed. A handful of keyboard players auditioned for the gig, and the fall tour began with both Hornsby (on piano) and Vince Welnick, formerly of the Tubes. The seven-man configuration continued through March 1992, with Welnick fully integrated into the ensemble. Hornsby then returned to his own recording and performing career, rejoining the Dead on accordion from time to time.

◆　　◆　　◆

VINCE WELNICK: In the material sense, [joining the Grateful Dead] changed me from a barn dweller to a ranch owner within six months. It seemed like being around Jerry and the boys, every day was like Christmas, or every year was like winning the lottery.

But in a more important sense—in the spiritual realm, and the musical realm—how it changed me was the encouragement I got from the band members to strive to do things I had never really done much of before. For instance, singing lead. I didn't do much of that with the Tubes. Bobby continually gave me the nod to do solos, which was gratifying.

It really opened me up to a lot of diverse styles of music. Bobby and Jerry and Phil's writing ran the gamut of everything—Jerry doing this simple and beautiful music, and Bobby and Phil providing different kinds of styles that were sometimes complicated but sometimes completely innovative. It allowed me to play with more diversity than ever before.

It also taught me that rock 'n' roll isn't a beauty

contest. I've never seen a more unconditionally loving audience, never played before as large a one as with the Grateful Dead. They weren't a bunch of shag pharaohs wearing spandex pants—that wasn't the key to the deal at all. The music created an environment for a whole culture that transcended many generations.

I've often wondered how it felt to you, walking into the middle of this insanely huge scene where the audience was so uncritically adoring of the band. . . .

It was the culmination of a vision I had when I was eleven, riding my Schwinn Stingray down Mulberry Street in Phoenix, Arizona. I stopped under a streetlight in the middle of the night and I saw this sea of humanity with their arms stretched out, and I was standing on a stage. I'd seen it a few times with the Tubes, but where it really made my hair stand up was the first time I was out on the summer tour with the Dead and we were playing outdoors in the daylight and you could see them all. There were thousands and thousands, and it was exactly what I saw in my vision as a kid. It was great—it was hard to hold back the tears.

I never cried so much for joy as [I did] playing in the Grateful Dead. With Todd Rundgren I'd get moved to tears, and sometimes with the Tubes I'd get elated to tears. But never so many times hearing music—particularly Jerry's—have I been so deeply moved by a musical experience.

◆　　◆　　◆

Welnick brought a fun-loving pop sensibility to the Grateful Dead. He prompted the revival of "Here Comes Sunshine" (from the 1973 album *Wake of the Flood*, not performed since February 1974) and tried to get the band to revive "The Golden Road (to Unlimited Devotion)," the single from the band's 1967 debut album. (Welnick performed both songs with his side band, the Affordables, in a handful of gigs while he was a member of the Dead.) He shared a love of Beatle music with his new bandmates, and at Welnick's urging the Dead played "Lucy in the Sky with Diamonds," "Rain," and "Tomorrow Never Knows" with some regularity in the last couple of years. "Tomorrow Never Knows" was coupled with The Who's "Baba O'Reilly," with Welnick singing lead on the latter.

A more vigorous Grateful Dead might have been more adventurous in their use of these cover songs. "Tomorrow Never Knows," for example, is a masterpiece of psychedelia and would have been a mindblower emerging from the depths of a second-set jam. But it only ever appeared in tandem with "Baba O'Reilly," and only once did the pairing show up anywhere but the encore.

◆　　◆　　◆

MIKAL GILMORE (*Rolling Stone*): Actually, to tell you the truth, the Dead's audience was frequently the part of those shows that I liked the best. For me, the band's music had lost much of its best edge and momentum several years before, which isn't to say they still weren't a protean or considerable ensemble; certainly I saw passages in various shows that were simply extraordinary. Plus, there was never a time I saw the Grateful Dead when I didn't appreciate that I was watching a band that clearly understood the meaning of playing together from the perspective of the long haul, with both a sense of history and a hard-won, deeply-held sense of fraternity. As a result, it was plain that the group understood not just the meaning of the words it sang, but also the meaning of the music itself . . . as a way of talking to one another, and as if music were the language of their fellowship, and therefore their history. That sort of experience—watching and hearing a band that had seen a long, hard, glorious, and matchless road, and that had learned to hold together and forge music as the bond of their affiliation—is the sort of deeply moving pleasure that, unfortunately, we encounter too little in the history of rock 'n' roll.

In every Dead show I saw, there was always a moment when it became plain that the audience's participation in these gatherings—and its sanction of the band—was as much the purpose of the shows as was the musical performance. As often as not, I found that moment in the band's reading of Buddy Holly's "Not Fade Away." There came a point toward the song's end when all the instrumental color and momentum would fall away—when the percussion and keyboards and guitars dropped out—and the band would just be singing, in their wonder-

JOHN ROTTET

KEYBOARDIST VINCE WELNICK, 1993.

ful roughhewn harmonies, to the crowd: "You know our love will not fade away. . . ."

"You know our love will not fade away!" the crowd would sing back to the band as one.

It would go on like that, the two bodies of this misfit community singing hard to one another, caught up in an awareness that they were bound to each other in a wonderful yet horribly risky way: As long as the one was there, the other would keep a hope. But if one should fall. . . .

◆　◆　◆

Garcia collapsed with exhaustion again in August 1992, forcing the cancellation of twenty-three dates, including the entire fall tour. By the end of 1993, Deadhead conversation pits were abuzz with concern about the increasing rigidity of set structures and an increasingly evident (to many people) decline in Garcia's onstage engagement. More and more fans complained that the band was just going through the motions, but at the same time, more and more fans attended shows in larger and larger venues. Clearly, large numbers of people were getting what they wanted from the Grateful Dead experience, and just as clearly, Garcia was disengaging.

From my vantage point as the producer of the "Grateful Dead Hour," whose principal source of material is concert tapes, the music did indeed suffer in those last few years. The last ten years saw a decline in flexibility, variety, and convincing improvisational interaction. The repertoire remained fairly broad, but fixed song sequences began to line up four or five deep in the nineties. Certain songs settled into specific places in the two-set structure of the Grateful Dead concert. This process predated the twentieth anniversary—Phil Lesh complained in 1982 that the band's concert format had been ossifying for years—but by the early nineties, some veteran listeners found it depressingly easy to predict what was to come, given the opening number of a set.

As Garcia's withdrawal became more obvious—and more controversial among the fans—the other members of the band seemed to work harder to compensate. Lesh, in particular, reinvigorated his songwriting ("Wave to the Wind," "If the Shoe Fits," "Childhood's End") and also his singing. I re-

member bursting into tears at the Oakland Coliseum on December 9, 1994, when Lesh sang "Broken Arrow" (a Robbie Robertson song that Lesh became interested in after hearing Rod Stewart's version on the radio), just because it was far and away the most *committed* delivery of any vocal I'd heard that night.

Another alarming sign was the installation of TelePrompTers on stage near the end of 1994. Given the frequency of various band members' verbal lapses onstage, the idea of cue cards or prompters had been a running gag for years—but when confronted with the reality, some fans were alarmed.

WELNICK: The TelePrompTers, contrary to popular belief, are very rarely on. How can you predict what song to put up when we don't even know what we're going to play? It's only in cases like a special request or when we drag a song out that hasn't been done very often and we need some lyrical help on it. It also helps with something like "Visions of Johanna," because there just aren't enough hours in the day to review all these lyrics. So this enables us to drag songs out from the past and do obscure tunes. But very little of the catalog is there. "I Want to Tell You" was on the TelePrompTer, and so was "Days Between." I think most of the new ones are probably on there. You can also run chord charts on them.

◆　◆　◆

One thing that did improve steadily over the last decade of the Dead's existence was the quality of the audio and visual production. Outdoor gigs in stadiums and "sheds" were augmented with video, and the Dead made sure they had the newest computer-assisted effects at their disposal. Lighting designer Candace Brightman created striking odd metal-framed screens above the stage and covered the speaker arrays with colorful scrims upon which her projections played. On some tours, video crews would gather footage outside the show and add those images to the projections in that evening's show. Coupled with state-of-the-art sound, the Dead managed to make their large-scale concerts reasonable artistic experiences.

"Went to the well but the water was dry
Dipped my bucket in the clear blue sky

Looked in the bottom and what did I see
The whole damned world looking back at me"

The summer tour of 1995 was plagued by an almost Biblical series of catastrophes, natural and social. Eyewitnesses reported unprecedented numbers of people outside the venues, begging for tickets, spare change, and drugs; lightning struck several fans in Washington, DC; a deck collapsed at a Missouri campground packed with Deadheads, injuring dozens; and most alarmingly, the second of two concerts at Deer Creek in Noblesville, Indiana, was cancelled after hundreds of people tore down a fence and charged into the theater.

Manager Cameron Sears, in a radio interview a couple of days after the incident, said, "We don't feel comfortable putting police and security, and ultimately members of our audience, at risk. It's not right, and it's not acceptable, and it's not something that we consider to be in the spirit of the Grateful Dead.

"The band has exhausted almost all of its attempts at trying to make a safe environment for people to come hear them perform," Sears continued. "We realize that there's a lot of great people that make up our audience, and we also realize that there's a very vocal minority that make it very difficult for us to have shows take place—at Deer Creek, probably the most appalling thing that we had to witness was the fact that there were people *inside* the facility cheering people on to break in to the concert, as well as *helping* them tear down the fence."

◆　◆　◆

LESH: Maybe it was like a pre-resonance of the event to come. Sometimes events of a certain magnitude have forerunner events that sort of pop up, and if you read 'em right you can see that maybe there's something big coming.

It's a ripple in time, kind of. Let's say that Jerry's death was a massive psychic event for a lot of people. Something that's that intense may form ripples in time that go out in either direction—pre-shocks, as opposed to aftershocks. That's just one way of looking at it. It did seem to get a lot more intense there before the end.

Also, maybe the music was fading because of the situation onstage and that's why the other level had come to the fore. After all, as we do know, the music *was* fading.

◆　◆　◆

". . . gave the best we had to give
How much we'll never know . . ."

After that fateful summer 1995 tour, Garcia checked himself into the Betty Ford Clinic in an effort to conquer his heroin addiction. According to news reports, he checked himself out halfway through the program and returned to his Marin County home. He then slipped into another facility in nearby Forest Knolls, and it was there that he died of a heart attack on the morning of August 9, 1995.

The press was almost universally kind to Garcia after he died. A handful of pundits took the opportunity to bash the sixties by characterizing Garcia as an avatar of moral turpitude and pronouncing his death a fitting end to a misbegotten generation—but for the most part, the coverage was positive.

RICHARD GEHR (*Village Voice*): No band ever took so many musical risks night after night, tour after tour, year after year, generation after generation. Garcia developed an ever-evolving musical palette that connected Earl Scruggs, Django Reinhardt, Chuck Berry, and Ornette Coleman. Yet his solos—rambling guitar narratives of mythical scale, lyrical wit, and emotional risk—always bore his immediately recognizable signature, warm and earthy phrases also as subtly alien as his right paw print. It's difficult to imagine another contemporary musician transforming the landscape of American music with as quicksilver an alchemy as Garcia. As much chemical substance as pop star, he turned the subject-object relationship of listener and artist upsidedown, reflecting back each auditor's best self in an impossibly bemused and knowing voice, and guitar notes as dear as precious metal. He was an Armstrong, a Coltrane, a Miles . . . a Garcia.

BLAIR JACKSON: Jerry would be going along in a certain way, and he'd reach a fork in the road—and he would always take the less predictable direction, someplace he hadn't gone before. So even if he played the same song three times in a row, like in the studio, he would always come to that same fork and he would have to take a different path than he had taken the previous time, just because that's the way he was, constitutionally. It raised the stakes in a way, because there's so much to grab out there.

JON PARELES (*The New York Times*): He played the way a dolphin swims with its school; his guitar lines would glide out, shimmer and gambol in the sunlight, then blend into the group as if nothing had happened.

◆　◆　◆

Garcia was "a mess," as one family member admitted, through most of the last fifteen years of his life. But the notion that he was a role model for drug abuse is as vile a canard as any I've heard; I know not a soul who was anything but heartbroken at the sight of this brilliant, eloquent, soulful performer staring at the floor through entire tours while precious little musical magic escaped his perimeter.

"If I knew the way
I would take you home"

VINCE WELNICK: I didn't think I'd be surprised when Jerry died, but it turned out I was very surprised. I was in denial for the longest time. The more the realization sunk in, the more depressed and morose I got about it. For a good long while I could barely get out of bed.

It was the end of my world as I knew it. It affected me more than anything that's ever happened in my life. The passing of my own mother came as a relief, because she suffered so much. But when Jerry died, I felt like I had died along with him. A big part of my soul went to hell for a long while and just about never came back. It was the worst time I've been through in my entire life—the winter of my total discontent.

I always felt like I was too sensitive to live in a world like this, but then when I got around Jerry and [the Dead] I realized that there is a place for love and understanding and peace and harmony. A beautiful world had come back, and when Jerry died it ended, as far as I was concerned. I couldn't talk myself out of the fact that my life was just over at that point.

I kept thinking how Jerry would have wanted

everyone to continue on and be happy, you know, but I just couldn't manage it. I was completely distraught, and I hit rock bottom. For a while I didn't think there was any coming back. But my friends—and especially my wife, Lori—hung in when nobody could be around me and I couldn't be around anybody else. She just refused to believe that that was really my lot in life, even though I couldn't see it. She kept telling me, "It's going to be okay, you'll get over it."

Eventually, it started to take, and now I am happy to say that in a way, it kind of forced me to do some things that I had never done before, like strike out completely on my own and work it out. I figure I'm probably stronger than ever before because of it, although I still have a hard time listening to the music and hearing Jerry sing without breaking down. I think time will heal that, too.

◆　◆　◆

RITA HURAULT

THE PROCESSION MARCHED AROUND THE FIELD AND THROUGH THE CROWD TO THE STAGE AT THE POLO FIELD IN GOLDEN GATE PARK AUGUST 13, 1995. DEBORAH KOONS GARCIA (LEFT FOREGROUND), PHIL LESH (BEHIND HER WITH DRUM).

CLOSE-UP OF THE SHRINE AT THE JERRY GARCIA MEMORIAL, SAN FRANCISCO AUGUST 13, 1995. FANS DEPOSITED PICTURES, POEMS, BEADS, FLOWERS, BUDS, AND ALL SORTS OF RELICS ON THE ALTAR DURING THE DAY-LONG CELEBRATION.

GOLDIE RUSH: The end of the Grateful Dead's live performances hurts my heart and gut. A loss of innocence, a fun thing gone. I will miss that clear high vibration only those guys could produce—those golden times when we were all playing in the band together and it seemed like we could change the world, make a difference, break through to something awesome and wonderful and pure and true. And we did. And we will.

CANDACE BRIGHTMAN (Grateful Dead lighting designer): [The Dead world was] one place I could go and be perfectly happy without taking drugs or otherwise denying reality—with my feet on the ground. That's gone now, and that's a real drag. It continued to work right up until the very end.

DAVID DODD (librarian): I now feel an occasional wash of intense sadness, just knowing that I will never see another Grateful Dead concert. For me, those concerts were the high church for my soul.

The concerts allowed me to connect my spiritual, emotional, intellectual, and physical beings in a way not available elsewhere. But I know that it's my responsibility to find ways to make all these aspects of my life connect *without* the Dead, and they've shown me lots of ways to do so.

BARLOW: I've always felt about my songwriting like I was dealing in a lost wax-casting process. I always start out with a melody line; sometimes it ended up being the melody line, and sometimes it didn't. I would create a bunch of lyrics around it, and then maybe Weir would trot in something else, and the original wax that those lyrics had been formed around would be melted away by the brass that would be fitted in there by the musician.

I think about the Grateful Dead that way now: The Deadheads are the biological layer that's encrusted itself around the sunken ship. The Dead are dead; the Deadheads are not.

210

KEN FRIEDMAN

BOB WEIR SPEAKS AT THE GARCIA MEMORIAL AUGUST 13, 1995.

ADAMS: My concern now is: Where am I going to go to feel that sense of community? Although I'm certainly in touch with a lot more Deadheads than most people are, being in touch with individual Deadheads is not the same as being in a room with thousands of them simultaneously. I wonder where I'll see those familiar faces in the crowd again. I wonder where I will feel that incredible sense of solidarity with others.

SUSAN DOBRA (scholar): It's like waking from a dream, but the waking has become more the dream; it becomes more and more of a delicate effort to hold the memory of that pure reality we all experienced for what seems now to have been a brief, fleeting moment in time. I feel an incredible challenge—an urgency, even—to manifest the essence of what we realized in concert with each other in a collective unfolding vision born of the lessons we learned there. I feel an ethical and spiritual obligation to carry it on, to bring to fruition what that old man and his friends blessed us with a peek of, graced us with the musical alchemical formula for.

BRUCE HORNSBY: It's hard to identify what constitutes "the end." They've said it's the end, but I'm just not so sure I'm ready to say they'll never play together again. If they all play together and it's not called the Grateful Dead, that doesn't mean sort of spiritually it's not the Dead. That whole attitude and mind-set and approach to playing will continue. There's a whole new strain of younger bands very much coming out of this spirit that was originated and defined by the Dead. If "the end" is "not playing with Garcia," well certainly that's done in this life. But I don't really see it having ended. Hell, this summer [1996] there's going to be a tour [Mickey Hart's Mystery Box, Bob Weir and Ratdog, Hornsby and his band, Los Lobos, Hot Tuna, et al.]. Just 'cause maybe it's not named the Grateful Dead doesn't mean it's not the Dead in spirit.

SENATOR PATRICK LEAHY: The outpouring of grief was very genuine. I think a lot of people feel, "Thank goodness we had the experience." Life is going to go on, of course, but the experience was worth it in the meantime.

I go to a lot of concerts of different types, everything from opera to rock. I love music, always have. But I'm not sure there's going to be anything where I'm going to have quite this experience, and the ex-

perience of closeness with my sons. I'm not going to try to seek something as a substitute, 'cause I don't think there is one. I'd rather hold the joy of the memory.

DICK LATVALA (Grateful Dead vault archivist): I think more and more people are going to pick up on this and see that something really was happening here, and they are going to learn about it by reading and talking to people who know about these things. I just hope that all of us who know something about this don't ever compromise and start trying to make any of the information easier for the outer public. There's no way you can explain what it's like to someone who hasn't done it. It's like explaining an LSD experience to someone who's never done it, or an orgasm to someone who never had one, or blindness to someone who's never been blind.

STEVE BROWN (filmmaker): I think it's sad that people won't have that in-person experience of being able to plug into it directly with their friends and the creators of that music. That energy is going to be sorely missed by all humanity. But the music still will exist for those people who seek it out and those people who remember it fondly, and those people will share it forever.

GARY LAMBERT: It happened sooner than any of us would have liked, but I don't see it as the end of the Grateful Dead any more than I see the mortal conclusion of Duke Ellington's life being the end of Duke Ellington, or of Beethoven's life being the end of Beethoven. The music is eternal, the influence will probably be enormous and widespread, and we also have musicians who are now going to diverge and maybe occasionally converge, and do marvelous creative things with the rest of their lives.

HART: Grateful Dead will never end! The Grateful Dead will live as long as the songs are played, and as long as the memory is here on Earth.

The spirit of the Grateful Dead is in my music, because I am. I go on, and I honor the past and I continue inventing. That's what the Grateful Dead is all about: invention, ingenuity, and playing hard and trying to find some spiritual end to all this instead of just a series of notes. I try to make it feel good to me, and in that way I think the Grateful Dead will continue.

JON McINTIRE: It makes me want to be certain

212

VINCE WELNICK, BOB WEIR, AND JERRY GARCIA SING THE NATIONAL ANTHEM AT CANDLESTICK PARK IN SAN FRANCISCO, OPENING DAY 1993.

that it is not the end of the Grateful Dead essence. It makes me feel more personally responsible for the continuation of some very important dreams that are possible and wholesome to bring to bear, by such tools as the Rex Foundation. Not falling for pat answers. Something about trust in life, in the benevolent forces of what we call life.

ALAN TRIST: Endings are beginnings. Personally, the "end of the Grateful Dead," which folklore will tell you is an oxymoron, has given me new life—and while saddened by the sense of loss, I am intrigued by the onset of new possibilities. After all, we're all still young, and something has to be figured out for New Year's Eve [1999]—symbolically, I mean, as to more of the good stuff. I'm depending on it.

SUE SWANSON: I have had to grow up and I've had to create alternatives in my life and fulfill them. The end of the Grateful Dead has given all of us an opportunity to fulfill our own dreams.

JOHN DWORK: End of the Grateful Dead? The Grateful Dead's music is so deeply programmed into my neurons, my DNA, that as long as I walk this earth the Grateful Dead experience lives.

CAROLYN GARCIA: That's good determination to hear. I think there's a tremendous amount of work to do, and we've been shown that creative work pays off in the long run. I don't think we need that lesson over again, but everybody's got to attend to their own creativity. That's what it means to me.

It's always a percentage deal. It's like throwing out pot seeds: only some of them come up, but the ones that come up can be pretty cool.

The mill of creation: I hope it never shuts down.

◆　　◆　　◆

MCNALLY: Three days after Jerry died I went by a store where I am known, and a twelve-year-old boy asked me, "Did you work with Jerry?" and such questions. When he heard that I did he went,

"Cool," as twelve-year-olds will. And this emotion went through me that said, "Yeah, I was part of the most amazing ride in American history. I was at the party."

HUNTER: The Grateful Dead is far from ended. It's taking a sharp left turn into cyberspace. Watch for developments. The [World Wide Web] site is about to be truly utilized. It's just a beautifully dressed corpse at the moment, but watch out.

What do you think the musical legacy of the Grateful Dead is?

LESH: I would hope a certain open-mindedness among musicians, a willingness to take risks, a willingness to experiment. A willingness to juxtapose disparate elements.

"I used to be a guy who'd go see a movie three or four times; I had that thing of wanting to repeat experiences. The Grateful Dead completely changed that. I don't want repeat experiences in my life. I practically never see a movie more than once. I want everything to be new, and the Grateful Dead did that for me."
—BLAIR JACKSON

◆　　◆　　◆

213

GRATEFUL DEAD AT SHORELINE AMPHITHEATER, 1993. LIGHTING DESIGN BY CANDACE BRIGHTMAN.

BILL SMYTHE

BILL SMYTHE

LAST SONG, LAST SHOW—SOLDIER FIELD IN CHICAGO, JULY 9, 1993.

214

How did the Grateful Dead change music?

ROBERT HUNTER: By introducing total self-indulgence to a heretofore rigid format notion of what pop music could be.

JON McINTIRE: They definitely helped to change the *business* in really basic ways. They refused to follow the formulas for success, and put the emphasis totally on the instinctual musical development. Everything else was secondary, or tertiary, or not even in consideration. Business was never the driving aspect until later on, and even then it wasn't really business, but just addiction to affluence. Even so, they never played the formula for success, even when they were fulfilling the need to remain affluent. It made it a pleasure to be a manager, because I could create my own game. I didn't have to play the music business game.

GERRIT GRAHAM: They stayed true to themselves and they did what they did on their own terms.

They invented themselves in a way that was satisfactory to them.

HENRY KAISER (guitarist): The Grateful Dead showed by example that it was possible to be anti-commercial but still be a commercial success—that you didn't have to sell out very much at all, in playing the music that you want to play, to make a living at it.

STEVE SILBERMAN: They demonstrated that there's actually a huge audience for "difficult" music—music that asks for the total involvement of the listener: mind, body, and soul. By tempering their excursions into space with the accumulated wisdom of the blues, bluegrass, jazz, and ballad traditions, they created an original idiom that was both visceral and subtle, timeless and perennially new. As multiculturally savvy citizens of the twentieth century, they played all the musics of the world as one great instrument. Is it any wonder that what spoke through that instrument was something like the voice of God?

JON McINTIRE: They combined more musical forms and influences than anyone I know. Mostly American, but the world—they brought in stuff from everywhere. Branford Marsalis said, "Those guys have really big ears!"

ALAN TRIST: They brought together the roots of American music, explored the limits of audio technology and live improvisation, pioneered high quality audio reproduction in large arenas, and gave new meaning to the idea of music as festival.

BRUCE HORNSBY: To me the Grateful Dead had a great combination of elements that they're not given credit for in certain circles. The combination was very powerful: fifty or sixty great songs. That's not unique—there are lots of bands with great songs—but the other part of the combination was their approach to playing those songs: it was sort of

SUSANA MILLMAN

MAKING THE "HELL IN A BUCKET" VIDEO, 1987.

an open-ended, improvisatory, exploratory attitude toward those songs. They'd have a song, but they were always into pushing it and fooling with it. A growing organism, a Grateful Dead song, ever evolving. So to me, the combination of the fact that they had a bunch of great ones, and their approach to those songs that made the songs not static, always changing and always growing—that made the songs breathe—was a great combination. Very powerful, to me. They brought this improvisatory spirit to a popular song context. That, to me, is how they changed popular music.

MICKEY HART: It served us all well—the band, the audience, and hopefully humanity. This band was about the raising of consciousness. It looked like a rock 'n' roll band, but the road it was headed in was not a road of hits. It was a different kind of road. We did it with everything we had; we put our lives on the line. A magnificent creation.

STEVE BROWN: They gave you more than you usually get from a band playing a tune. You could close your eyes and go on long journeys with them, and twist and turn down all kinds of places that you normally couldn't go with a musical band. It was a kind of improvisational experience that I think probably will never be equaled by any other band.

215

JOHN DWORK: As electrified visionary artists, they were able to externalize the experience that one has in a shamanic, psychedelic, or transcendent experience, and in doing so were able to show other musicians how to share with much larger audiences the connection with god-consciousness that was previously limited to the experience of the musicians and the few people surrounding them.

DAVID DODD: The Grateful Dead brought something of the egoless Gamelan aesthetic into American music. They were a *group*—not "Jerry Garcia and the Grateful Dead," not "Pigpen and the Grateful Dead." The sound they created is instantly identifiable, yet impossible to pigeonhole. They made something new, but always respected the traditions that contributed to their own form.

JON McINTIRE: They buttressed that jazz-improv-identified "trust in the moment" by going out there and doing extraordinary experiments. When they paid off, it was as glorious as anything I have ever heard. And all the more glorious because it wasn't planned: It happened. The Grateful Dead was very now-oriented.

Bobby [Weir] called Grateful Dead "The band that dares to be wrong."

VINCE WELNICK: I got to experience true improvisation—like drums and space, which I believe is true improvisation: Nothing was preconceived, and nothing was structured whatsoever. It didn't start with a lick or a groove—it was completely off the top of your head.

BOB BRALOVE: The Grateful Dead set up situations where the issue at hand was not so much an issue of delivering a prescription, but of connecting to the music. Getting inspiration from the music and having the ego dissolve and *being* the music is what is magic, what is universal about music. It is the thing that connects rock 'n' roll to trance music to symphonies to everything—it's just being lost in the moment.

REBECCA ADAMS: For me, the most important

thing about their shows was their ritual structure—building to a formless peak and then ending with raucous rock 'n' roll—allowing us to get comfortable, then letting us each go off on our own explorations, and finally bringing us back together again for a celebration of our unity. I never cared what songs they played. For me the trajectory of the show was the important part of the experience.

BERNIE BILDMAN: I don't think they *changed* it, but rather brought us back to the age-old concept that music is best served when we have an egoless conversation. Much as the best basketball team is not predicated on how great each individual talent is, but rather how they *communicate* with each other. Energy levels not possible before became touchable in a way we never thought feasible. This concept is what they reminded me of each time they "got it together." It was truly alchemy.

REBECCA ADAMS: Perhaps their most lasting contribution will be having changed the way music is

KEN FRIEDMAN

BONNIE RAITT JOINS THE GARCIA BAND AT THE GREEK THEATER IN BERKELEY.

KEN FRIEDMAN

NEIL YOUNG JOINS THE DEAD FOR "FOREVER YOUNG" AT THE TRIBUTE TO BILL GRAHAM IN GOLDEN GATE PARK NOVEMBER 3, 1991. GRAHAM DIED IN A HELICOPTER CRASH ON OCTOBER 25, 1991.

consumed. Although other bands have had loyal followers, I don't think anyone can challenge Deadheads for first place. Now a lot of bands and performers have fans who will follow them from place to place, but it was Deadheads' example that set the pace.

BLAIR JACKSON: You occasionally hear the Dave Matthewses and Phishes talking about how they derived a certain looseness of approach to it, and obviously the way the Dead related to their fans is the envy of many a band—although it's something that's very hard to duplicate, obviously. But musically, I don't think they've had that much of an impact. Even at their most popular, the Grateful Dead were still a fringe band; they were still crazy guys who played half an hour of space music at every show they did. Nothing ever changed that, and nothing ever changed the fact that they played ballads that bored a lot of people, and weird shuffles that a lot of people couldn't dance to. It was always a very singular, odd thing. Those of us who have

seen the escalation of it through the years were fooled into thinking it was some big thing, but even at its biggest it was still incredibly idiosyncratic, and weird, and small in the grand scheme of things. It was never a mass phenomenon.

I'm going to be really interested to see how the Dead are regarded in fifty or sixty years, without the distraction of the whole Deadhead phenomenon. I think it's going to come to be regarded pretty well. I especially think that some of that sixty-eight to sixty-nine stuff is going to be up there with John Coltrane—when people have a better idea what was involved, the immensity of this music. It was really something to behold.

"They made the world safe for improvisational music with a backbeat."
—DENNIS McNALLY

JERRY GARCIA BAND AT THE WARFIELD IN SAN FRANCISCO.

SOURCES

The interviews, books, articles, and broadcast features listed below are the primary sources of text in *Playing in the Band*, but the music of the Grateful Dead is the "big picture" from which this portrait is drawn. I have been attending concerts regularly since 1972, but I have been able to hear Grateful Dead live shows going all the way back to the band's first year and coming all the way from Alaska, Europe, and Egypt, thanks to the dedication of the tapers. These indefatigable microphone-wielders neither dance nor cheer nor sing along, so that others may share Grateful Dead shows at other times in other places; they are true folk historians.

BOOKS

Davis, Clive. *Clive: Inside the Record Business.* New York: William Morrow, 1975.

England '72 "Book of the Dead" (tour book). London: Warner Bros. Records, 1972.

Grushkin, Paul, Bassett, Cynthia, and Grushkin, Jonas. *Grateful Dead: The Official Book of the Dead Heads.* New York: William Morrow, 1983.

Jackson, Blair. *Grateful Dead: The Music Never Stopped.* New York: Delilah Books, 1983.

Petersen, Robert M. *Far Away Radios.* Privately printed, available through the Grateful Dead.

Reich, Charles, and Wenner, Jann. *Garcia: The Rolling Stone Interview.* San Francisco: Straight Arrow, 1972.

ARTICLES

Abbott, Lee. "The Jerry Garcia Feature." *Feature,* March 1979.

Bashe, Philip. "What a Long Strange Trip It's Been." *Good Times,* April 22–May 5, 1980.

Block, Adam. "Garcia on Garcia '77." *BAM,* December 1977 and January 1978.

Brown, Larry, and Gregg, Jonathan. "Dead Drummer Feeling Good." *New Paper,* January 17–24, 1979.

Caen, Herb. *San Francisco Chronicle,* March 19, 1969.

Campbell, Mary. *Indianapolis Star,* January 23, 1979.

Carroll, Jon. Interview with Jerry Garcia. *Playboy Guide/Electronic Entertainment*, Spring/Summer 1982.

Crowe, Cameron. "Grateful Dead Flee Big Business." *Circus*, 1973.

———. "Grateful Dead Show Off New Bodies." *Creem*, January 1974.

———. Interview with Bob Weir. *Rock*, June 30, 1973.

Damsker, Matt. *The Bulletin*, August 29, 1980.

Doerschuk, Bob. "Brent Mydland: Taking Over Keyboards for the Grateful Dead." *Keyboard*, September 1982.

Eisenhart, Mary. "Robert Hunter: Songs of Innocence, Songs of Experience." *The Golden Road*, Summer 1984.

Fong-Torres, Ben. "Fifteen Years Dead." *Rolling Stone*, August 7, 1980.

Fricke, David. "The Dead Survive the '70s." *Circus Weekly*, January 16, 1979.

———. "The Dead Celebrate 15 Long Strange Years. . . ." *Circus*, 1980.

Garbarini, Vic. "In Search of the Grateful Dead." *Musician*, October 1981.

Grissim, John. *Rolling Stone*, November 6, 1975.

Haas, Charles. "Still Grateful After All These Years." *New West*, December 17, 1979.

Hall, John. "In the Year of Deliverance." *Unicorn Times*, 1977.

Hunt, Ken. Interviews with Jerry Garcia, Tom Constanten, and John Barlow. *Swing '51*, numbers 6 and 8.

Iero, Cheech, and Perry, Charles. Interview with Bill Kreutzmann and Mickey Hart. *Modern Drummer*, August-September 1981.

Interview with Phil Lesh. *Zig Zag*, number 46.

Interviews with Phil Lesh and Mickey Hart. *Comstock Lode*, Autumn 1981.

Jackson, Blair. "The Dead's Link with the Heads." *The Golden Road*, Fall 1984.

———. "Out in the Wild Blue Yonder with Tom Constanten." *The Golden Road*, Summer 1984.

——— and Erokan, Dennis. "Bill Graham: Rock's Godfather, Part II," *BAM*, February 1, 1979.

Jarvis, Elena. "Fountain Valley Alums Discuss Days with 'The Dead.'" *Gazette Telegraph* (Colorado Springs), August 15, 1980.

Kates, Marcy. *Wall Street Journal*, November 22, 1974.

Lydon, Michael. "The Grateful Dead." *Rolling Stone*, August 23, 1969.

McClanahan, Ed. "Grateful Dead I Have Known." *Playboy*, March 1972.

McKaie, Andy. "Bob 'Ace' Weir Steps Out." *Crawdaddy*, September 1972.

McNamara, Robert. "The Oldest-Established Permanent Floating Rock Band in the World." *New York Daily News*, July 25, 1982.

Peacock, Steve. "Jerry Garcia in London." *Rock*, July 17, 1972.

Perry, Charles. "A New Life for the Grateful Dead." *Rolling Stone*, November 22, 1973.

Peters, Catherine. "Dead Ahead." *Pacific Sun*, February 13–19, 1981.

Rense, Rip. "The Dead Dance in the Land of Chance." *Los Angeles Herald Examiner*, March 29, 1983.

Robins, Wayne. *Newsday*, March 16, 1980.

Rowland, Mark. "Still Dead After All These Years." *The Real Paper*, June 28, 1980.

Sievert, Jon. "Jerry Garcia . . . Patriarch of the San Francisco Sound." *Guitar Player*, August 1981.

Stix, John. "Bob Weir's Rhythm Guitar Lesson." *Guitar World*, May 1982.

Swenson, John. *Rolling Stone*, 1978.

Tamarkin, Jeff. *The Aquarian*, July 9–16, 1980.

Weitzman, Steve. *The Drummer*, October 2, 1973.

Wilcock, Donald E. *Times Record* (Glen Falls, New York), n.d.

Young, Charles M. "The Awakening of the Dead." *Rolling Stone*, June 16, 1977.

BROADCAST INTERVIEWS

Berardini, Tony. Interviews with Mickey Hart, Bill Kreutzmann, Dan Healy. Broadcast nationally during Grateful Dead concert, November 24, 1978.

Ellerbee, Linda. "Not Ready for Prime Time News" segment on the Grateful Dead. "NBC News Overnight," December 1983.

Fong-Torres, Ben. Interview with Jerry Garcia. Broadcast on KFOG "Archive Hour," 1984.

Sources

Frost, Vance, and Wanger, Michael. History of Grateful Dead, with interviews and music. Broadcast on KSAN, 1969.

Krassner, Paul. May 1984 interview with Jerry Garcia. Broadcast nationally during Grateful Dead concert, June 21, 1984.

Kurtis, Bill. Interview with Jerry Garcia, Bill Graham, Grace Slick. "CBS Morning News," July 17, 1974.

Letterman, David. Interview with Jerry Garcia and Bob Weir. "Late Night with David Letterman" (NBC), April 13, 1982.

O'Shea, Steve. Interview with Jerry Garcia, Bill Kreutzmann, Ron "Pigpen" McKernan, Bob Weir. Broadcast on KFRC, 1966 (courtesy of Tom Ordon).

"Portrait of a Legend" (syndicated television program). Interviews with Jerry Garcia, Mickey Hart, Bob Weir.

Shalit, Gene. Interview with Jerry Garcia. "Today Show" (NBC), March 12, 1981.

Simmons, Bonnie. Interview with Jerry Garcia. Broadcast on KSAN, January 23, 1976.

Snyder, Tom. Interview with Jerry Garcia, Mickey Hart, Bill Kreutzmann, Bob Weir. "Tomorrow" (NBC), May 7, 1981.

"Videowest's Backstage Pass" (syndicated television program). Interviews with Grateful Dead members and Dan Healy, 1981.

Wexler, Paul, and Salditch, Mark. Interview with Mickey Hart, Bob Weir. Broadcast on KSAN during Grateful Dead concert, July 18, 1976.

221

DAVID GANS has been following the music of the Grateful Dead since early 1972. Since then he has attended the requisite number of concerts and collected enough hours of tape to qualify as a serious Deadhead. Since dropping out of San José State University in the early 1970s, he has worked as a musician, traveling trainer/troubleshooter for a computerized entertainment ticketing concern, and a freelance writer/photojournalist. He is currently a senior editor of *Record* magazine and music editor of *Mix*, the recording industry magazine. He lives in Oakland, California.

PETER SIMON is a freelance photographer and author who lives primarily on the East Coast. Among the eight books he has published are *Decent Exposures* (Wingbow Press, 1974); *Carly Simon Complete* (Knopf, 1975); *Reggae Bloodlines* (with Stephen Davis, Doubleday, 1977); *On the Vineyard* (Doubleday, 1980); and *Reggae International* (with Stephen Davis, Knopf, 1983). Specializing in photojournalism, alternative lifestyles, and music, his photographs have appeared in *Rolling Stone, Musician, Life, Time, Newsweek,* the *Village Voice, Atlantic Monthly, Islands Magazine, Popular Photography,* and *New Age*. He became a Deadhead in 1970 and has followed the group far and wide since.

TOP: HASTILY ASSEMBLED GROUP TABLEAU FOR *LIVE DEAD* CENTERFOLD, WITH FRONT AND BACK COVER PAINTINGS AND RANDOM OBJECTS AS PROPS. PIGPEN IS IN THE DRIVER'S SEAT, AND AROUND HIM ARE *(CLOCKWISE FROM FAR LEFT)* WEIR, TC, GARCIA, LESH, AND HART. *ABOVE:* WEIR AND DONNA GODCHAUX POSE AS LOOKALIKES DURING THE 1972 EUROPE TOUR. *RIGHT:* WEIR AND KREUTZMANN SHOW OFF SUITS CUSTOM MADE BY NUDIE, THE HOLLYWOOD TAILOR FAMOUS FOR BRIGHTLY DECORATED CREATIONS POPULAR WITH COUNTRY MUSIC STARS, JUST BEFORE THE START OF THE EUROPE '72 TOUR.

ANNIE LEIBOVITZ

ANNIE LEIBOVITZ

ANNIE LEIBOVITZ

ABOVE: GARCIA AND DAUGHTER ANNABELLE, 1973

TOP: THE GRATEFUL DEAD "FAMILY"—BAND, CREW, STAFF, ASSOCIATED BUSINESSES, SPOUSES, BABIES, AND A PARENT OR TWO—IN SAN RAFAEL, OCTOBER 1973 *ABOVE:* PREPARING FOR A SOUND CHECK WHILE ON THE ROAD IN 1973. STEVE PARISH HELPS KREUTZMANN ADJUST HIS DRUM KIT.

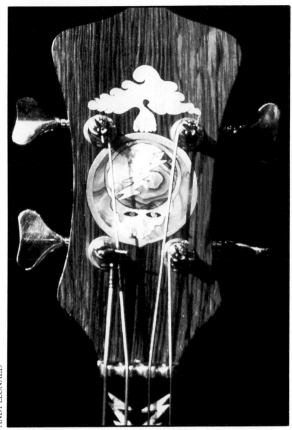

ANDY LEONARD

BOB MARKS

TOP: PEGHEAD OF PHIL LESH'S ULTRA-HIGH-TECH 1974 BASS, WITH THE ALEMBIC SYMBOL AND THE GRATEFUL DEAD SKULL AND LIGHTNING BOLT LOGO INLAID IN MOTHER-OF-PEARL *ABOVE*: A CLEAN-SHAVEN GARCIA BACKED BY THE "WALL OF SOUND" AT THE OAKLAND COLISEUM, JUNE 8, 1974

OVERLEAF: ROSES IN PERIL. WINTERLAND, OCTOBER 1974. ABOVE: ONE OF ONLY FOUR PUBLIC APPEARANCES DURING THEIR NINETEEN-MONTH "RETIREMENT," THE DEAD, BILLED AS JERRY GARCIA AND FRIENDS, PERFORM AT AN ALL-STAR BENEFIT CONCERT AT SAN FRANCISCO'S KEZAR STADIUM ON MARCH 23, 1975. IN ADDITION TO THE RE-ENLISTED MICKEY HART, THE LINEUP INCLUDES KEYBOARDISTS MERL SAUNDERS (FOREGROUND) AND NED LAGIN (REAR).

ABOVE: IT'S NOT A LITTLE TV, IT'S A TUNING METER. *LEFT:* ALTERNATE SHOT FROM THE *GO TO HEAVEN* COVER SESSION, 1979

GARCIA AND DEADHEADS, JULY 1980

ANNIE LEIBOVITZ

GARCIA AND COMEDIAN AL FRANKEN TAPING "JERRY'S KIDS TELETHON" SKETCHES FOR CLOSED-CIRCUIT SIMULCAST OF HALLOWEEN 1980 GIG FROM RADIO CITY MUSIC HALL.

ROGER RESSMEYER

ROGER RESSMEYER

LEFT: UNIDENTIFIED RECORDING ENGINEER AFTER WORKING TWENTY-THREE SHOWS IN FIVE WEEKS IN SAN FRANCISCO AND NEW YORK, SEPTEMBER AND OCTOBER, 1980

KEN FRIEDMAN

RICHARD McCAFFREY

ABOVE: RAM ROD PREPARES THE TAR JUST BEFORE HANDING IT TO MICKEY HART DURING THE DRUM DUET.

LEFT: BILL GRAHAM, AS FATHER TIME, RIDES A GIANT MUSHROOM AND THROWS ROSES AS MIDNIGHT APPROACHES AT THE OAKLAND AUDITORIUM, DECEMBER 31, 1982.

ABOVE: PHIL LESH SINGS AT THE GREEK THEATRE IN BERKELEY, JULY 15, 1984. BY THE END OF THE YEAR HE HAD A MIKE OF HIS OWN, ENDING A DECADE OF LEAVING THE SINGING TO OTHERS. *LEFT:* LESH DONS FORMAL ATTIRE TO ATTEND THE PREMIERE OF A NEW OPERA BY HIS MENTOR, LUCIANO BERIO, IN SALZBURG, AUSTRIA, IN AUGUST 1984. THE EVENING INCLUDED A REUNION BETWEEN THE COMPOSER AND HIS PROTÉGÉ, WHO TOLD BERIO HE WAS "STILL GRATEFUL DEADING."